JOSSEY-BASS™
A Wiley Brand

T0342496

Growing Your Membership

91 Ways to Recruit & Retain More Members

Scott C. Stevenson, Editor

WILEY

978-1-118-69054-3   ISBN

978-1-118-70390-8   ISBN (online)

Growing Your Membership
91 Ways to Recruit & Retain More Members

Published by

Stevenson, Inc.

P.O. Box 4528 • Sioux City, Iowa • 51104
Phone 712.239.3010 • Fax 712.239.2166
www.stevensoninc.com

Growing Your Membership

91 Ways to Recruit & Retain More Members

TABLE OF CONTENTS

ARTICLE DESIGNATION KEY: ▨ RECRUITMENT ▨ RETENTION

TABLE OF CONTENTS

ARTICLE DESIGNATION KEY: ▨ RECRUITMENT ▨ RETENTION

Growing Your Membership

91 Ways to Recruit & Retain More Members

1. What's Your Plan for Growing Membership?

Down economy? So what. Don't let external factors impede your efforts to expand membership numbers. Identify growth strategies that will allow you to overcome the odds. Here are examples of membership expansion strategies to include in brainstorming sessions:

- Kick off a member-recruit-a-member campaign with a goal and special perks for members who produce, or consider making it a contest.

- Get a sponsor to underwrite the cost of several new limited-time member benefits you can use to make a special push for joining now.

- Come up with an appealing one-time event, then make the cost to attend cheaper by purchasing a one-year membership. The Art Institute of Chicago, for instance, once attracted a Monet exhibit that resulted in a drastic increase in membership.

- Offer a six-month membership at a reduced rate and with fewer benefits.

- Offer a one-time multiple year membership at a slightly reduced rate.

- Launch a workplace contest. Whoever recruits the most colleagues from his/her place of work wins a prize.

2. Identify Strategies for Retaining First-time Members

When you have the good fortune to generate new members, teach them the habit of membership renewal. Getting a membership renewal is key to a long-term relationship. That's why it's critical to identify strategies aimed at securing that first renewal.

Examples of first renewal strategies may include:

1. **Nurture first-year members appropriately.** Incorporate steps year-round to communicate with first-year members in special ways. Let them know they're noticed and appreciated. Publicize membership in your newsletter, on your website and in other ways.

2. **Engage first-year members.** Involve them in activities that interest them. See that they get personal invitations to participate in activities or events you think may be of interest to them. Get longtime members to help in that process.

3. **Begin renewal process in the third quarter.** Offer renewal options that make it as easy as possible (e.g., online renewal, quarterly installments, credit card).

3. Double Recruitment Success By Reaching Out to Couples

Ever identify volunteer projects to benefit your member-based organization that reach out to couples, married or otherwise?

Inviting couples to volunteer — whether they are both members, just one is a member or they are prospective members — provides them with the opportunity to be together as they serve a common effort. It also offers a ready-made comfort level of knowing the person with whom each is working.

More importantly, volunteering as a couple can be an enriching, relationship-strengthening experience.

To initiate a program that encourages couples to volunteer:

1. **Identify volunteer opportunities that most appeal to couples.** Create a checklist of projects ranging from simple to more complex — filing, staffing the front desk or an event registration table, co-chairing an event, team phoning or solicitation, serving as hosts or tour guides and more.

2. **Develop a plan to market volunteer projects to couples.** Consider an ad program that reaches out to couples and lists volunteer opportunities. Recruit a couple to head-up your couples program and enlist others. Do a feature story on a couple already volunteering for your cause to illustrate the rewards of couples volunteering.

3. **Work with existing couples to keep them invigorated.** Once you have couples involved, find out which projects are most rewarding for them and weed out those that are not. Ask how you can support their work.

4. **Identify unique ways to recognize couples' efforts.** Host periodic appreciation events for all couples volunteers. Offer special bus trips or discounts to restaurants. Make being couples volunteers attractive to those who have not yet stepped forward.

91 Ways to Recruit & Retain More Members

4. To Attract New Recruits, Serve Existing Members Well ▨ ▨

Bonnie Grady, President/CEO, Chamber of Commerce of the Mid-Ohio Valley (Parkersburg, WV), says membership organizations that put recruitment as the No. 1 priority should consider putting retention there instead.

Unless you are a new organization, you have members already, Grady says. Focus first on serving them well in order to make membership look attractive to prospective members. "If you're doing a good job of making your members feel valued, and you promote those achievements," she says, "others will notice and want to be part of your organization."

Here are a few ways Grady says work to keep existing members happy:

✓ **Create and promote programs that cause prospective members to seek you out.** "You have to have specific benefits that speak to prospective members. Then you can begin to promote those benefits. For example, we've launched a new program called the Nonprofit Executives' Roundtable. Nonprofit organizations — both members and nonmembers — are invited to a 90-minute session where they share news of upcoming projects and events, identify resources, address concerns and share best practices. Since nonprofit boards are made up of local business reps, we're casting a wide net. We expect to see more local nonprofits joining the chamber as a result of this new initiative."

✓ **Create payoffs for your volunteers.** "Our points-based rewards system in my former chamber helped our ambassadors set their own goals and achieve them. We've started a similar program at the MOV Chamber and we call the volunteers Chamber Champions. Now the membership development committee has asked if they can have a points system, too!"

✓ **Listen, listen and listen.** "The simplest conversation can provide clues to what prospective members fear the most, what they want more than anything else and what they are willing to do to get it."

Source: Bonnie Grady, President/CEO, Chamber of Commerce of the Mid-Ohio Valley, Parkersburg, WV. Phone (304) 422-3588. E-mail: bgrady@movchamber.org

5. Get Entire Staff on Board to Boost Recruitment Success ▨

The Center for Nonprofit Management (Dallas, TX) supports nonprofit organizations throughout greater North Texas by advising, educating and offering tools and best practices to nonprofit boards, staff and volunteers. While the center focuses on providing agency memberships, the organization also offers individual memberships.

Katie Edwards, director of marketing, says the center has 580 agency and 72 individual members. "We mostly recruit agency members as membership benefits apply to all staff and board of the nonprofit," Edwards says. Individual memberships are reserved for persons interested in the nonprofit sector who are not affiliated with a specific nonprofit.

"We serve more than 5,000 nonprofit staff and board members through a variety of services like our seminars and training, consulting services and Opportunity 501, our non-profit job listing," she says of the center's outreach methods. "The majority of our outreach goes to this audience, those individuals who are currently using our services, but are not members. Most of our outreach is through e-marketing like e-newsletters and blast e-mails.

"Our website is another great outreach tool as many people learn about us for the first time through the Web," Edwards says. The center's website highlights member benefits and offers an online registration option that allows persons to join immediately.

Edwards offers tips on recruiting individual and agency memberships:

✓ Increase membership benefits and their perceived value. This means learning about what they value, what they want out of their membership and adding benefits that they see as attractive.

✓ Communicate valuable information. Keep your organization top-of-mind for members, but be sure to send valuable communication. Think about what it is that they find most valuable and useful.

✓ Educate all staff and board on membership so that everyone is recruiting new members. For example, if a client registers for a class with the education department, the education staff should understand the membership savings and recommend to that client that they become members in order to receive discounted pricing.

Source: Katie Edwards, Director of Marketing, Center of Nonprofit Management, Dallas, TX. Phone (214) 826-3470. E-mail: Edwards@cnmdallas.org. Website: www.cnmdallas.org

6. 15 Ways to Retain Members

To keep current members and bring back those whose memberships have lapsed:

1. Send lapsed members a Welcome Back letter offering a special renewal rate. Include an invitation to an upcoming event for them and a guest.

2. Include news on your website about new and current members.

3. Ask inactive/former members to events.

4. Match existing members with new members to share a ride to meetings.

5. Gather a list of lapsed members and ask them to participate in a focus group to better your organization.

6. Send a survey asking lapsed/inactive members for ideas to improve your organization. Conduct a call night to contact this group for suggestions.

7. Send a monthly e-mail message to active and inactive members coinciding with the mailing of your newsletter to reinforce what it will bring them and to capture the attention of lapsed members.

8. When a membership goal is achieved, announce it on your website to relay that your membership is growing.

9. When a former member attends an event, make personal contact. After inviting former members to an event, be sure greeters and board members make a special effort to welcome them.

10. If persons are absent from a meeting, send a handwritten note or make a call to tell them they were missed.

11. Keep your organization a warm, welcoming environment. Create a space where members are welcome to just hang out when they drop by.

12. Introduce roundtable luncheons where active members are matched with inactive ones. Host brainstorming meetings asking active members for ideas on retaining lapsed members.

13. Combine monthly meetings with a local fun event such as a concert or ball game. Hold your regular meeting, then attend an area event as a group.

14. Send active and lapsed members post-meeting updates, focusing on positive outcomes of the meetings and sharing personal stories from active members.

15. Allow members to put memberships on hold when necessary and return to active membership when able.

7. Shine the Spotlight on Superstar Members

Whom should you feature in your next member spotlight? At the Technical Association of the Pulp and Paper Industry (TAPPI) of Norcross, GA, they seek the best and brightest stars among their membership to tell their tales in the spotlight.

Serving 20,000-plus professionals in the paper, packaging and converting industry, TAPPI showcases members on its website at www.tappi.org/spotlight.

Rich Lapin, marketing manager, says that with the spotlight, they seek to cover all types of members at different levels of experience.

The online member feature includes the member's photo, a brief biography and a link to a more extensive bio. The bio features information on the member's background and affiliation to TAPPI, plus a question-and-answer section in which the member shares more about his/her experience with TAPPI. In addition to the website, TAPPI also includes the spotlighted member in one or more of its e-newsletters.

"Exemplary individuals of TAPPI who we hold out as the shining stars of achievement are featured in the member spotlight," says Rich Lapin, marketing manager at TAPPI. "These are exemplary members in their membership, their energy level and what they've been able to achieve. They truly are TAPPI's shining stars of achievement."

For TAPPI, the member spotlight serves a dual purpose, says Lapin: to build awareness of the membership organization and to honor extraordinary members.

Whether you're starting a new member spotlight feature or refining an existing one, Lapin shares questions to ask to help the member share his/her story:

- Why did you decide to join?
- Describe your involvement with our organization.
- How has membership helped you in your career pursuits?
- Tell us about your interests outside of the organization and your professional life.
- Can you share a unique or fun fact about yourself?
- Please share any closing sentiments about your relationship with the organization.

Source: Rich Lapin, Marketing Manager, Norcross, GA. Phone (770) 209-7290. E-mail: rlapin@tappi.org. Website: www.tappi.org

8. Award-winning Membership Campaign Builds on Successful Marketing Effort

Looking for inspiration to launch your next direct mail effort? Look to the direct mail membership campaign for the Denver Zoo (Denver, CO).

Not only did the effort help add more than 5,000 members and raise nearly $300,000, it earned industry accolades, taking first place in the Direct Marketing Association of St. Louis' (St. Louis, MO) Arrow Awards for its Membership Acquisition Campaign. DMA-St. Louis is a professional society of members with an interest in the practice, study and teaching of direct marketing.

Zoo staff worked with Membership Consultants (St. Louis, MO), to create a five-piece membership mailer mirroring the zoo's marketing campaign, "Every Time You Visit You Help Animals." Membership campaign artwork also mimicked that used in the marketing campaign, creating a branded appeal and saving on costs.

Mary Bradley, director of membership services, says the mailer centered on the Year of the Frog, a designation by zoos and aquariums across the country. Showing up in a bright green envelope that featured the flap and the address window on the same side, allowing the other side to be used entirely for artwork, the packet contained:

✓ A two-sided letter from Bradley promoting a 10-percent discount to all new members regardless of level;

✓ A 6 X 8 1/2-inch brochure boasting artwork, colored photographs and details about the benefits of membership;

✓ A reply piece and return envelope.

To track the appeal, which involved dropping 150,000 pieces in one week, each piece was coded with zoo lists, Bradley says. "Twelve weeks out we compared all the folks who joined as of the drop date and then compared that to our mailing lists (e.g., lapsed member lists, lists traded with cultural organizations in Denver, and various magazine lists). We were able to determine we saw a 3.62 percent response rate or 5,430 new memberships."

The appeal cost more than $98,000 and netted $293,220. Costs included consultant fee ($19,500); printing/mailing cost ($34,474) and postage ($27,461).

Sources: Mary Bradley, Director of Membership Services, Denver Zoo, Denver, CO. Phone (303) 376-4875.
E-mail: mbradley@denverzoo.org
Dana Hines, President & CEO, Membership Consultants, St. Louis, MO. Phone (314) 771-4664, ext. 105.
E-mail: dana@membership-consultants.com

Denver Zoo's award-winning direct mail membership appeal included, from top, a letter about benefits; colorful envelope; reply card, return envelope (not shown) and zoo brochure (not shown).

Content not available in this edition

Content not available in this edition

Content not available in this edition

9. Help Current Members Stay on Board ▬

Some research indicates it's seven times more costly to recruit a new member than to retain an existing one. That's why, during these turbulent economic times, it makes sense to do whatever is possible to retain current members.

Evaluate your renewal procedures to determine how you can retain a higher percentage of current members. Explore renewal strategies such as:

✓ Offering a two-year membership for the price of one.

✓ Allowing memberships to be paid over a 12-month period through electronic funds transfer (EFT) or automatic credit card deductions.

✓ Creating a tiered membership that offers basic membership at a lower price and higher-level memberships that include more perks.

Your goal should be to make membership renewal more palatable in light of financial constraints facing today's members.

10. Offer Member Testimonials ▬ ▬

Out to recruit more members? Consider the ways in which testimonials from existing members can give rise to new ones.

In addition to serving as your best sales force, testimonials provide yet another way for members to become involved and more committed to your organization.

Explore the various ways in which your current members' testimonials can be used to recruit others:

1. **Have existing members speak to a group of prospective members.** Whether it's a gathering with the expressed purpose of recruiting members or a speaking engagement for a civic organization provided by one of your members, incorporate public testimonials into your recruitment efforts.

2. **Include printed testimonials in membership brochures.** Used sparingly, brief testimonials, along with a photo of those providing them, can provide an effective means of inviting others to join your ranks.

3. **Use existing members to initiate a membership recruitment campaign.** Before you kick off your campaign, spend time with recruiters discussing why others would benefit from membership. Doing this will provide your recruiters with helpful testimonial messages and will help motivate them to bring in new members as well.

4. **Pitch the media an occasional human interest story that includes member testimonials.** Whatever your story's focus, incorporate quotes from existing members that enforce the worthiness of your organization and why it's great to be a member.

11. Valentine-themed Event Draws New Members ▬ ▬

Dovetail a special event with a much-loved holiday to create a memorable, member-building occasion.

For three years, the Isabella Stewart Gardner Museum (Boston, MA) has hosted a Valentine's Day event, treating members and potential new members to an evening of elegance.

At the 2009 Venetian Valentine event, the museum treated 264 guests to live jazz, cocktails, fine art and romance. Throughout the evening, romantic self-guided tours of the art collection were available to guests, romantic delicacies such as oysters and chocolate-dipped strawberries were served and a jazz quartet played music in the flowering courtyard.

Nonmembers paid $90/person and $175/couple, which included a year of museum membership. Members paid $65/person and $125/couple. The museum sold 87 new memberships in one evening, says Brittany Duncan, museum publicist.

Hosting a Valentine's-related event can create an opportunity to promote membership at a time of the year that can typically be slow for new memberships.

Follow these tips to promoting membership at your next event:

✓ Create an event with wide appeal that capitalizes on the unique aspects of your venue or organization. Because of its history and atmosphere, the Isabella Stewart Gardner Museum encourages personal connections with art — so a Valentine's event that allows couples to share a special evening in the intimate setting is especially appropriate.

✓ Focus on the event as an opportunity to attract new members through creative advertising and promotion to reach and appeal to a wide audience.

✓ Set the price competitively with other local Valentine's Day options.

Source: Brittany Duncan, Publicist, Marketing & Communications, Isabella Stewart Gardner Museum, Boston, MA. Website: www.gardnermuseum.org

ARTICLE DESIGNATION KEY: ▬ RECRUITMENT ▬ RETENTION

91 Ways to Recruit & Retain More Members

12. Creative Techniques Show How to Attract Members ▨

People join museums and art centers for the collections, but ancillary membership benefits can often be the difference between simply reading the brochure and writing the check.

To draw more members to your venue, consider these creative and unusual perks:

Performing and fine arts — The Seattle Art Museum (Seattle, WA) offers a unique twist on reciprocal programs with a performing and fine arts companion pass that offers discounts to institutions like the Seattle Opera, Symphony and International Film Festival.

Art rental — The Seattle Art Museum also offers members more than 1,000 works of art for rental or no-interest installment purchase, starting at $50 a month.

Research library — Whether titled academics or curious amateurs, the Field Museum (Chicago, IL) offers members use of its extensive and renowned research library.

Members-only website — Members of Smithsonian Affiliate institutions across the country can bring the splendors of the world's largest museum and research complex into their homes through a password-protected, members-only website.

Ecological conservation — Through a $45 membership-extension package in collaboration with The Reclamation Project, members of Miami Science Museum (Miami, FL) can have a mangrove planted in their name in Biscayne Bay and receive a native tree to plant at home.

Themed incentives — Consider themed member incentives such as:

- Education: College planning, scholarships or grant programs.
- Discounts: Membership-based deals for auto clubs, hotels, airlines, cell phone services, online retail stores and more.
- Insurance: Life, disability, dental, vision, health, home, car or pet insurance.
- Home: Moving service discounts, real estate affinity programs, mortgage and refinancing services.
- Counseling: legal, financial, retirement and other counseling.
- Travel: Cruise, tour or theme park discounts.

13. New Membership Levels Offer Affordability ▨ ▨

Consider offering new membership levels that will not only attract new members, but will offer cost-effective options for a broader audience.

Staff of the Western Reserve Historical Society (WRHS) of Cleveland, OH, recently developed new low-cost membership levels to aid its growing membership of 2,600.

"To address the concerns of our members and be sensitive to the financial burdens this economy is placing on people, we came up with a few alternatives that we introduced in fall 2009," says Kim Fleischman, director of individual support. "We scaled back or ramped up certain membership options to accommodate current and future members.... We are becoming more user friendly and developing levels of membership that benefit our constituents and their needs."

WRHS staff introduced the following new membership levels:

- **Armchair Historian.** For $25 per year, a new member can opt to become an Armchair Historian, a scaled-back version of standard membership. The level offers guest passes for one-time admission, discounts on purchases at museum stores and electronic updates of museum news.

Half the cost of the $50 Individual level, it does not include such things as a subscription to the newsletter, reciprocity to other institutions or discounted admission to special programs as full membership offers.

- **Senior Couple.** This new $60 level, which allows those 62 years or older to join and receive admission for two adults, is designed for seniors who asked for a reduced rate and visit often, but do not have offspring nearby who will be attending WRHS.

- **Partner.** WRHS created the Partner Membership level to accommodate supporters of the museum who found the Fellow level at $500 per year out of reach. The new level offers members the opportunity to act as a Sustaining Member of the organization with fewer benefits for only $250 per year — half the rate of a full Fellow membership.

Source: Kimberly Fleischman, Director of Individual Support, and Becky Carlino, Director of Community Engagement, Western Reserve Historical Society, Cleveland, OH. Phone (216) 721-5722. E-mail: bcarlino@wrhs.org. Website: www.wrhs.org

14. Added Benefits Can Boost Member Renewals ▬

Looking for a way to sweeten the pot for renewing members? Try setting up a multi-tiered program with added benefits for each additional year of membership.

You can let members know about the added benefits up front or at renewal. Informing them up front allows them to see that benefits will grow over time, along with their membership.

You can even offer an incentive to encourage members to pay for a multi-year membership. Letting them know at the time of renewal gives them incentive to renew and adds value to the membership.

15. Breakfast Orientation Meetings Serve More Than Eggs ▬ ▬

New members of the Kirkwood-Des Peres Area Chamber of Commerce (St. Louis, MO) enjoy information-packed orientation sessions over a casual weekday breakfast.

"Enjoying a meal together during a morning orientation helps to keep our new members informed on how they can make the most of their chamber investment," says Gina March, vice president of marketing for the chamber. "The more goods and services they can use to build their businesses, the more likely they are to feel a connection to us, and that affinity builds."

The chamber hosts the breakfast events three to four times a year.

"These breakfast events benefit members by providing information on what services and products the chamber offers," March says. "They also get to meet each staff person (who explains what she does), as well as all the ambassadors and board members. There is also considerable networking before and after the event. And, of course, free breakfast. In the last two years, our attendance has climbed dramatically from 40 in September 2007 to 110 this past June. Each event in between was better attended than the one before."

March shares four tips for organizing a successful breakfast orientation for members:

❑ Invite businesses that do not have early morning business hours to host the event. For example, she says, "Our local Red Robin Gourmet Burgers (which only serves lunch and dinner fare) has been thrilled to create a breakfast buffet for members attending the event."

❑ Get members personally involved in the process to invite newcomers to the event. Include existing members on your invitation list and get the word out in print and electronically. "New members want to learn all they can about getting involved," she says, "and veteran members want to network with new members."

❑ Invite a business to be the host sponsor. In the chamber's case, this means getting a two-minute infomercial and having a booth at the event. Sponsors pay $300 to host the event and receive other benefits, such as having their company's logo on fax/e-mail blasts and posted on the member orientation website.

❑ Don't create handouts for every event and service you offer. "It is a lot of copying and folder stuffing that is mostly useless," March says. "We learned the hard way by picking up all the folders people left behind or didn't take. Now we ask all members to get out their business card and hold it up for everyone to see. Then we tell them to hang on to their card and write every question, request or additional info they want on the back of it. We pick them up at the end of the event and follow up with each one of them."

Source: Gina March, Vice President of Marketing, Kirkwood-Des Peres Area Chamber of Commerce, Kirkwood, MO. Phone (314) 821-4161. E-mail: gina@thechamber.us

Content not available in this edition

16. Five Recruitment Strategies ▨

Here are five ways to increase your organization's membership by a hefty percentage:

1. Host a series of receptions, programs or tours targeted to individual businesses and their employees.

2. Coordinate a Kids Campaign. Children of members who recruit other kids (or families) get prizes.

3. Convince a foundation, business or individual to sponsor a 50 percent off introductory membership offer, paying half of newcomers' annual dues.

4. Coordinate a series of one-day membership campaigns targeting unique groups — left-handers, twins, vegetarians, the clergy and more.

5. Create a one-time reciprocal agreement with another organization: "Your members will be entitled to full membership in our organization for three months if ours are entitled to the same with your organization."

17. Techniques for Attracting the Younger Crowd ▨

The organization, Business and Professional Women/USA (BPW/USA) of Washington, DC, has an active and growing grassroots membership, more than 15,000 strong.

Growing stronger by meeting the needs of its members and other working women, the organization has taken specific steps to attract female members ages 18 to 35. Those steps include broadening its Web presence and offering career development to this age group.

BPW/USA's current focus is on outreach to young working women and women veterans, which includes having a presence on Facebook, MySpace and LinkedIn — popular social networking sites young adults often frequent.

"The main focus right now is utilizing and adapting technology to better suit the needs of the members by creating more online outlets for discussion and networking as well as resources and information," says Jennifer Pflasterer, manager of member satisfaction.

Taking steps to engage young members and potential members who readily use technology fosters creativity and conveys that your organization is in touch with young professionals, Pflasterer says.

In addition to using technology and the Web to connect with younger working women, BPW/USA membership management staff offer career-oriented services and challenges that address the needs of young female professionals, she adds. For instance, BPW/USA has a contest in which college students prepare a Web-based video that highlights the issues that their generation faces as they enter the workforce. The goal of the challenge is to get students to think about what types of issues they will encounter and where they may get support.

BPW/USA's Career Center allows its women and veterans to advance in their chosen careers and features employers that support women veterans and families while encouraging work-life effectiveness.

BPW/USA's Women Joining Forces program is specifically designed to offer veterans resources and networking opportunities as they are entering the civilian workforce, says Pflasterer.

Websites Connect Young People To Each Other, Your Organization

Attracting the younger generation to your membership organization means communicating on that generation's level.

Consider creating a presence on these and other trendy websites frequented by young people:

- **www.facebook.com** — Facebook is a social networking website where users can join networks organized by city, school, workplace or region to connect and interact with friends or acquaintances through user's personal profiles.

- **www.myspace.com** — MySpace is another social networking website offering an interactive approach to the user's network of friends. This site also offers personal profiles, blogs, groups and photo sharing.

- **www.linkedin.com** — LinkedIn is a business-oriented social networking site used primarily for professional networking.

"Organizations that are not directly related to women, but have women members, can use these methods to determine how the female demographic differs from males, and activity areas they may pursue in an effort to recruit more women," says Pflasterer.

"The issues faced by women today are the same as those of our mothers and grandmothers," she notes. "However, the means and experience to attract and reach them is different and will continue to change as time goes on. It is important to have the flexibility to adapt and update the activities, resources and methods of communication to meet the needs of diverse and ever-changing target groups."

Source: Jennifer Pflasterer, Manager of Member Satisfaction, Business and Professional Women, Washington, D.C. Phone (202) 293-1100. E-mail: jpflasterer@bpwusa.org

ARTICLE DESIGNATION KEY: ▨ RECRUITMENT ▨ RETENTION

18. Strategies That Build Loyalty ▬

Interested in building greater loyalty to your organization among volunteers, members, your board and other constituents? Check out these strategies, which will help do just that:

1. **Build meaningful traditions.** Annual ceremonies — whether with pomp and circumstance or a flair unique to your nonprofit — contribute to the bonding process of those affiliated with your organization.

2. **Instill camaraderie.** Building loyalty among colleagues and friends associated with your organization also strengthens agency loyalty.

3. **Make roles and events official.** Make it important to be appointed to a volunteer or board position. Introduce and publicize new members or appointed individuals. Present them with a certificate or lapel pin as part of their entry into your organizational family.

4. **Position your organization against the competition.** Although you should avoid doing it in a negative fashion, there is no better way to build instant loyalty than to position yourself against a rival. One potential downside: You may lose potential members who view you as someone from the other side.

5. **Tug at the heart strings.** Invoke dearly held memories linked to past times with your organization. Focus attention on a long-respected employee or board member for whom many have great admiration.

Organizational loyalty results in commitment, and commitment results in a willingness to contribute both time and resources. Examine ways in which you can work to build greater loyalty among your organization's constituency.

19. Obtain Feedback From Members Who Leave ▬

Learn from the members who leave your organization.

A personal phone call to persons who choose not to renew their membership can provide you with valuable feedback that can help you better serve existing members. The outreach effort may also cause the person to reconsider membership.

Staff with Western Home Furnishings Association (WHFA) of Roseville, CA, call each member who fails to renew membership 30 days after their renewal due date.

"Before we cancel a member, we have a phone call with them to determine the reason for leaving," says Kaprice Crawford, membership director. "The members will either tell our membership team it was an oversight, arrange for payments if they are struggling, or tell our sales team they will not be renewing and the reason why."

Typical reasons members give for not renewing include:

- The member company is going out of business.

- The member can no longer afford membership.

- A program they participated in has been discontinued.

- They only joined for one program and are not interested in joining others.

Staff created a report in Microsoft Excel detailing all member cancellations of the last five years. The report includes the member's name, location or territory, level of membership and the reason they give for not renewing. Members who do not respond to either the renewal invoice (sent 60 days before renewal deadline) or the phone call are labeled accordingly in the report.

The report is a useful tool for the association's staff, the membership director says. With the document, "I can see which territories are struggling geographically and we can put together prospecting strategies for that area, specific educational sessions for that area or regional business programs for the area. In addition, I can see what kinds of members are canceling. If a specific segment of membership is not finding value in the associations, then we can either eliminate this segment and not market to them anymore or we can tailor more programs, services and education towards this segment."

Crawford says they decided to conduct the follow-up efforts strictly by phone after attempts at using mailed and e-mailed exit surveys failed to provide a good response.

The statistical information has resulted in creation of a new staff position.

"Because of this report, I put into place a member service specialist whose job it is to initiate members into the association, explain all the programs and get the members immersed into the organization to try to guarantee renewal and value in membership," says Crawford. "She also is developing a more solid relationship with our members. Before this change, our membership development team was responsible for sales, service and renewal, and not enough time was spent on service. Our report told us so!"

Source: Kaprice Crawford, Membership Director, Western Home Furnishings Association, Roseville, CA. Phone (800) 422-3778. E-mail: kcrawford@whfa.org

20. Direct Mail Campaign Attracts Almost 2,000 New Members

Get more out of a major event by using it to raise awareness of your membership program.

Staff with The Barnes Foundation (Merion, PA) publicly announced architectural plans for its new building on Philadelphia's Ben Franklin Parkway. They used the opportunity to launch a membership campaign that would build toward the structure's 2012 grand opening by inviting a targeted group to join as founding members of The Barnes on the Parkway.

"Having managed direct mail campaigns for The Phillips Collection in Washington, D.C., Atlanta's High Museum of Art and the Philadelphia Museum of Art, where we were mailing more than 1.4 million pieces, I felt that mail is still a very important acquisition tool," says Mark Mills, The Barnes' director of individual giving and visitor services. "Prior to this, I also revamped The Barnes' membership pages and trained our visitor services team to start asking people to join when selling tickets."

Mills says the first direct mailing was a risk, since the foundation had not used direct mail before and had no past results to reference. "We tested a simple invitation-style membership mailing with, 'You're Invited' on the outer envelope," he says. "We kept costs low and projected that we would need 240 new memberships to break even and regain the initial investment. We also planned the package to arrive in homes the same week of the media coverage of the new building plans to ensure a two-hit campaign — press and mail."

The direct mail piece consisted of a four-page letter, brochure, reply form and business reply envelope. It offered a savings off regular membership rates, double the regular number of admission tickets and an invitation to an exclusive founding members reception to view the museum's collection, plans and architectural models for the new building.

Sent to 40,000 regional homes made up of ticket buyers and exchange lists, the mailing attracted nearly 1,000 new members and raised more than $110,000.

Officials sent 60,000 direct mail pieces in the second mailing and another 50,000 in a final mailing to additional recipients. The second mailing attracted 744 members and raised $80,000. In the first week of returns, the final mailing attracted 205 members and raised $27,000.

Mills says they outsourced the direct mail project to The Lukens Company (Arlington, VA), which designed the package and concept and provided mail services. The Barnes tracked the responses in-house using Raiser's Edge fundraising software by Blackbaud (Charleston, SC).

As the grand opening of the new building nears and momentum builds, Mills says, plans are to mail approximately 800,000 pieces over an eight-month time frame with a focus on member preview events, founding member status and the ability to see the building first.

Source: Mark Mills, Director of Individual Giving and Visitor Services, The Barnes Foundation, Merion, PA. Phone (215) 640-0171, ext. 17. E-mail: mmills@barnesfoundation.org

Unique Factors Make for Successful Campaign

Mark Mills, director of individual giving and visitor services at the Barnes Foundation (Merion, PA) attributes the success of its recent direct mail campaign to the combination of several factors, including:

✓ Other than small grassroots efforts, this was The Barnes' first active membership promotion.

✓ The Barnes' extraordinary collection of 181 Renoirs, 69 Cezannes, 59 Matisses, 46 Picassos and 2,000 other premier Impressionist and Post-impressionist works. "The Barnes is notorious for being difficult to get in to," Mills says. "The package promoted easier access to tickets for members and also created urgency for people to see it before the collection moves from its original location."

✓ The offer of discounted rates, a special event and founding member status.

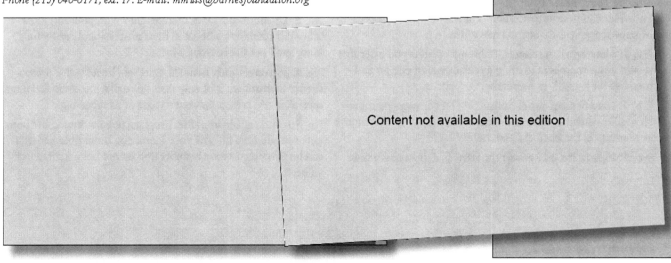

Content not available in this edition

21. Six Ways to Motivate Member Recruiters ▨▨

Nothing beats members recruiting other members, but member-get-a-member programs fall flat without sufficient enthusiasm and incentive. Here's what a number of organizations are doing to light a fire under member recruiters:

1. **Easy on the budget.** If money is tight, consider following the example of the American Statistical Association (Alexandria, VA), which avoids excessive prize expenditures by rewarding recruiting members with discounts on association products, services and educational programs.

2. **Make it unique.** The periodic table of elements throw blanket offered by the American Chemical Society (Washington, D.C.) not only suits member interests, it is offered exclusively through the membership campaign and is unavailable for purchase anywhere else.

3. **Everyone loves a raffle.** The American Sociological Society (Washington, D.C.) generates enthusiasm and participation with a grand prize, available to anyone signing at least one new member, attractive to members of all types and stripes — a $599 iPad tablet computer.

4. **Tiered rewards.** The American Medical Directors Association (Columbia, MD) encourages members to think big with four graduated levels of rewards: preferred members who bring in 1 to 4 members annually, select members who bring in 5 to 10, elite members who bring in 11 to 25 and premier members who bring in 26 or more members.

5. **Get local.** The Urban Land Institute (Washington, D.C.) brings member recruitment to the grassroots level by offering $1,000 prizes to the local chapters with the highest number and highest percentage of new members.

6. **Keep the prize points coming.** The Association for Computing Machinery (New York, NY) keeps members motivated with a veritable flood of prizes, offering gifts for the first referral, every other referral after that (e.g., third, fifth, seventh, etc.), and a special bonus prize for the 10th new member.

22. Give 10 Reasons to Join, Stay ▨▨ ▨▨

Highlight your top 10 reasons for returning to your membership organization again and again. One way to do so is with a takeaway card that you mail to members or that they can pick up to remind them how membership benefits them.

Here are ideas for creating your list:

No. 1: Membership bonds the family. Offer members specific examples of upcoming family-oriented events that could allow them to enjoy membership with their children or grandchildren.

No. 2: Educational opportunities. Focus on classes, tours or other learning-based offerings that could advance a member's knowledge of your organization or advance their own breadth of knowledge within their career or life.

No. 3: Sharing with friends. Point out options you offer that would allow members to bring a friend or sign one on as a member for a credit or discount.

No. 4: Networking opportunities. Spell out ways membership offers members a networking base to grow their business or contacts in the business community.

No. 5: Resources and research. Provide details about how membership can benefit them with research in specific areas. Cite useful members-only resources.

No. 6: Keeping and creating community jobs. Encourage membership by emphasizing how your organization provides the community with gainful employment. Offer details on how many people your organization employs and how membership benefits the community.

No. 7: Investment. Show your members how being a member is a good investment. Gathering all the benefits and reflecting that in monetary form can show members what a great value membership offers.

No. 8: Credentials. Does membership with your organization offer members a boost in their professional credentials? If so, spell out the reasons why.

No. 9: Members-only benefits. Spotlight benefits that are exclusive to members. Not only does this make members feel more special, it also creates enhanced value of membership.

No. 10: Intangible benefits. Emphasize what intangible benefits membership affords your members. Intangible benefits can be perceived-value benefits that do not have a monetary value.

23. Invite Nonmembers to Your Member Events

Women for Winesense (Napa, CA) — an education and networking membership organization for wine aficionados and professionals — offers monthly events at its chapters for members to meet, mingle and learn about fine wines.

These events also serve as effective membership builders, as members are encouraged to bring nonmembers as guests, says Karen Jess-Lindsley, president.

Jess-Lindsley notes that the organization has grown its membership to 715 with 12 active chapters without ever having held a membership drive. The member-invite-a-friend events, typically held at local restaurants or wineries, are a major factor in helping grow membership, she says. As an example of a typical event, Jess-Lindsley says the Napa/Sonoma chapter will offer a wine blending seminar where members can create their own Bordeaux blend and take home the bottle.

"Each chapter puts on these amazing events where people can taste and learn about wine," says Jess-Lindsley. "Once nonmembers see the discount that members are getting and the great events we offer, they're excited to join."

Source: Karen Jess-Lindsley, President, Women for Winesense, Napa, CA. Phone (800) 204-1616.
E-mail: Karen@lindsleyconsulting.com

24. Build Strong Recruitment Program From Ground Up

Take recruiting efforts back to the basics by retraining your board and other key persons on membership recruiting efforts.

A refresher course with one-on-one and group training will strengthen recruiting skills. Start with a brainstorming session that addresses the following:

- ❑ **Redeveloping goals.** Hold a strategic planning session to evaluate membership growth opportunities. Define a specific goal and steadfast steps to reach it. Develop a growth strategy that meets income needs to sustain and grow the organization.
- ❑ **Reviewing your prospect list.** Divide your list of prospects into manageable groups, sending information that caters to each group's interests in order to draw them into your membership. Maintain a current potential-member list and send information to them on a regular basis highlighting your member events.

- ❑ **Refining communication strategies.** Ask current members for testimonials that reflect your membership goals and aspirations to share in communications with potential members and in membership literature. Spotlight value-added benefits.
- ❑ **Streamlining your membership application process.** Find ways to refine the application process. Develop a process that is welcoming, easy and rewarding.

25. Awards and Rewards Help Recruit and Retain Members

An awards program can serve to reward your existing members and garner attention to grow your membership base.

Staff at Associate Builders and Contractors, Inc. (ABC) headquartered in Arlington, VA, know the importance of recruiting and retaining members. To encourage recruitment and retention among members in its 78 chapters with a combined membership of more than 24,000 firms, staff developed an awards program offering incentives to members through the Beam Club.

Under the Beam Club, first established in 1966, ABC members are recognized for their commitment to grow the association by rewarding them with valuable gifts.

"ABC National supports the membership recruitment efforts of our chapters with our Beam Club program which recognizes members for their efforts," says Doug Curtis, vice president of chapter services. "We purchase and provide the awards, so the chapters may recognize and reward members for their efforts. The awards are presented by the chapters."

Each member recruited is worth one point with points accruing year to year, advancing the member chapter to the next award level within the program. A member sponsor is enrolled in the Beam Club once five members are recruited.

Once 50 new members are recruited, the member receives national recognition by reaching the Beam Club Hall of Fame, with his/her name placed on the Hall of Fame plaque and chapter profiled in ABC's weekly electronic newsletter.

Club awards include plaques, lapel pins, shirts, jackets, watches, mantel clocks and more.

Source: Doug Curtis, Vice President of Chapter Services, Associate Builders and Contractors, Inc., Arlington, VA.
Phone (703) 812-2009. E-mail: curtis@abc.org. Website: www.abc.org

26. Recognize the Efforts of Long-distance Members ▬▬

While recognizing the efforts of members who may be assisting you from far-off locations is important to retaining them, doing that can be challenging.

Make time to create a menu of recognition strategies for these more distant members. Examples may include:

- A lapel pin or piece of jewelry that designates their special relationship to your organization.
- Scheduled phone calls to discuss business and unscheduled calls to pat them on the back.
- Posting information on your website noting their valuable contributions.

- Insider news that lets them know they're appreciated.
- Thank-you phone calls from higher-ups (board members, CEO, others).
- Publishing their names as VIMs (very important members).
- Placing an ad in their local newspaper that publicly recognizes them.
- Sending an occasional photo of events taking place at your organization.
- Mass-producing and sharing a DVD of a special event or ceremony.
- Sending a card and personal note at unexpected times.

27. Examine Why Members Leave ▬▬

If you've had a sudden drop in membership, don't just blame it on the economy and fail to seek a solution. Rather, consider the possible reasons for the drop, then take action to reverse the trend.

Gather your membership committee and ask these questions to find solutions to the dip in membership:

❑ Do our members feel that meetings are useful and engaging?

❑ Are members encouraged to speak at meetings and contribute to the greater good of our organization?

❑ Do members feel as though the organization's goals match their interests?

❑ Are members finding the meetings to be too time consuming?

❑ Does our nonprofit encourage diversity?

❑ Do members feel rewarded and feel as though they benefit from membership?

❑ Has membership become cliquish, appearing to be open to only a select group? How can we overcome that?

Find answers to these questions by polling members, hosting a member retreat or creating a clearly defined survey is a first solid step to reducing member attrition.

28. Keep Members Connected With a Full-service Help Line ▬▬

What better way to serve members than to make sure that help is just a phone call away?

"Our member help line is one of the best services we offer," says Cathy Kennedy, director of member development at the California Restaurant Association (CRA), Sacramento, CA. She describes the help line, which has operated for decades, as central to the work of the association. "Tip pooling, alcohol and beverage control, licensing, insurance, statistics — we take questions on everything you can imagine and answer them all."

A staff member who operates the help line full-time answers many of the questions. She forwards issues she cannot resolve to appropriate CRA staff. Answers to frequently asked questions have been developed in areas of common concern.

Because of the complexity of California regulatory law, the CRA also maintains, as part of its help line services, a partnership with a law firm specializing in restaurant labor law. Through this partnership, members receive 15 minutes of free labor advice a month. To make the most of that time, CRA staff generally conduct a pre-interview with the member and supply the attorney with a background report on the problem or question.

While access to the help line is restricted to normal business hours, an auto-form online component allows members to submit questions 24 hours a day.

Source: Cathy Kennedy, Director of Member Development, California Restaurant Association, Sacramento, CA. Phone (916) 447.5793. E-mail: Ckennedy@calrest.org

29. Show Your Gratitude With Member Appreciation Events

Member appreciation events are a great way to express gratitude to your members while boosting awareness of your membership program. For inspiration, check out these two approaches to member appreciation events offered by the Children's Museum of Richmond (Richmond, VA) and the Denver Bar Association (Denver, CO):

Children's Museum of Richmond's month-long member celebration, May 2010:

- **Member-only Evenings** — Every Thursday in May, 5:30-7:30 p.m., the museum was open exclusively to members and featured special entertainment.
- **Extended Member Mondays** — These day-long Monday events held in May included opportunities to meet players from the Flying Squirrels and get their autographs.
- **Bring a Friend for Free** — Every day in May, members could bring one free guest to the Children's Museum of Richmond.
- **Win a Pair of Bikes** — Each time members visited the museum in May, they were entered into a drawing to win a free adult and child's bike, courtesy of Fitness Resource in Richmond. The winning entry was drawn during the Members-Only Evening Event on Thursday, May 28.

Denver Bar Association Annual Member Appreciation Week, Monday, June 7 through Saturday, June 12, 2010:

- **Monday:** Henry Hall Memorial Golf Tournament
- **Tuesday:** Annual Awards Party at the Curtis Hotel; Job Search and Career Transition Support Group
- **Wednesday:** Seniors Spring Banquet at the University Club
- **Thursday:** New Member Mixer
- **Friday:** Tuesdays at the Bar: Mindfulness for Lawyers
- **Saturday:** Document Shredding Party and BBQ; Member Appreciation Night with the Colorado Rockies (Denver Bar Association members get a 25 percent discount on tickets.)

Use these suggestions to create a special week, month or season of benefits to reward current members. Be sure to spread the word before and during the celebration to entice people to sign on as members.

30. Techniques Help Catch the Eyes of Female Members

Since its inception in 1988, the Women's Institute for Financial Education (WIFE) of San Diego, CA, has attracted 55,000 members, most of whom are women seeking financial guidance. The organization, which educates women on financial planning, offers various membership levels with special perks that catch the eye of potential female members:

✓ **Basic Membership** — This $25 membership level includes tangibles including the organization's newsletter, the booklet 150 Ways to Save Taxes Through Life's Transitions, A Man is Not a Financial Plan™ bumper sticker, and the intangibles of feeling great about supporting the organization and helping to expand its sister organization Money Club.

✓ **Membership Donation Options** — Donation levels are offered in increments of $25 through $1,000 to allow members to empower the organization with funding.

- Premium Level 1 — Those supporting WIFE at the $100 level also receive the organization's exclusive Small Step Sandal pendant necklace.
- Premium Level 2 — This level at $250 includes an autographed copy of the founders' book: "It's More Than Money — It's Your Life: The New Money Club for Women."

Source: Ginita Wall, Director, Women's Institute for Financial Education, San Diego, CA. Phone (760) 736-1660. E-mail: GWall@wife.org. Website: www.wife.org

Promotions Appeal to Women

Ginita Wall, director of the Women's Institute for Financial Education (WIFE), San Diego, CA, shares perks and promotions that appeal most to female members:

- *Humor:* Giving out bumper stickers that say A Man is Not a Financial Plan™ reflects a sense of humor and intrigues other women to contact WIFE to learn more.
- *Gifts:* Offering member levels with various gifts that appeal to women, such as, the pendant draws in females.
- *Sensibilities:* In today's economy, more women are looking for financial freedom. The tools, resources and books offered by WIFE that are geared to this goal attract many members.
- *Publicity:* The best way to get women members, says Wall, is through publicity. "When WIFE is featured in articles on the Internet, the organization receives a lot of hits at the website," she says. "We maintain good relationships with many journalists, so they turn to us for information and quotes, with attribution in their pieces. We include journalists (with permission, of course) in our distribution list for our monthly webletter, and the webletter content often sparks their interest in doing an article Print media is also helpful, since people can clip articles and refer to them, and television and radio are somewhat less helpful."

31. Creative Partnership Has Members Walking in the Door

Looking for a way to boost your membership? Try thinking about an alternate appeal your facility might have.

That's what officials with the Louisville Zoo (Louisville, KY) did when they teamed up with Norton Healthcare (Louisville, KY) to create the Healthy Walking Club for Zoo Walkers in 1995.

"We charge a yearly sponsorship fee, which provides use of the zoo in a creative way," says Terri Lenahan-Downs, zoo sponsorship manager. "As part of their sponsorship, Norton Healthcare paid for walking signage throughout the zoo that includes healthy tips for walkers who follow the 1.2 mile loop."

Here's how the partnership works to benefit both non-profit organizations:

People sign up for the club at no cost through Norton Healthcare and receive the Best Foot Forward kit, membership card, route and distance information for the zoo and other sites, plus Norton Healthcare's bi-monthly Get Healthy! magazine.

Walking club members get free entrance to the zoo to walk 8-9:30 a.m. Mondays-Saturdays March 1-Oct. 31 and 6-8 p.m. Thursdays and Fridays in June, July and August. Zoo exhibits are not open during morning walking club hours.

Lenahan-Downs cites benefits of the partnership: "We have a lot of hills, so it gives walkers a good workout. It provides a safe alternative to walking in a park or on roads. It gives our members an added perk since it's free. It also introduces walking club members to the zoo who may not otherwise visit and hopefully encourages them to want to come back during normal zoo hours and even join the zoo."

Some 2,500 people belong to the walking club, with five to 30 walking at the zoo each day, depending on the weather.

Source: Terri Lenahan-Downs, Sponsorship Manager, The Louisville Zoo, Louisville, KY. Phone (502) 238-5330. E-mail: Terri.Lenahan-Downs@louisvilleky.gov

32. 10 Steps to Keep Members Involved and Engaged

Officials with the National Association of Health Underwriters (Arlington, VA) have developed an extensive list of retention ideas to help staff and chapters focus on keeping their valuable members. Illana Maze, senior vice president of marketing and development, shares 10 of their most successful retention tips:

1. **Involve new members in association activities immediately.** Have them participate in an event as soon as they show an interest in your chapter. Ask them to co-chair a committee or coordinate a small activity in the early stages of membership. Initiating their activity into your membership will ensure their success as a member.

2. **Realize the best time to retain members is before they show signs of dissatisfaction.** Make sure members know you care. If they start missing meetings or become less involved in activities, call to find out why before it becomes a chronic situation.

3. **Send a member profile form to new members** to gain information and to secure the best ways to contact that member.

4. **Add at least one extra contact during their first year of membership** for members recruited during a membership drive.

5. **Conduct focus groups by phone.** Ask members with various experience levels to focus on needs of a small segment, such as a new member focus group. Send focus group participants an agenda and set of rules. Take attendance; let everyone know who is attending, and make a list of who speaks so you know whom to ask for input.

6. **Communicate successes to members regularly.** If you have exciting news to share, send an e-mail blast to your membership to engage and energize them.

7. **Conduct e-mail surveys of important questions and issues as they arise.**

8. **Color code correspondence so members can quickly identify types of information they receive.** For example, use one color paper or ink for educational information another for legislative information and so on.

9. **Increase meeting attendance** by featuring an interview with the meeting's keynote speaker in the publication that comes out a month before the meeting.

10. **Remember there are only two forms of currency you can use to pay members: recognition and tradition!** Look for any opportunity to recognize a member's contribution. Create a tradition in your chapter and recognize those who uphold the tradition.

Source: Illana Maze, Senior Vice President of Marketing and Development, National Association of Health Underwriters, Arlington, VA. Phone (703) 276-3811. E-mail: mgibson@nahu.org

33. Chapter Membership Challenge: 13 Ways to Recruit, Retain New Members ▓▓▓ ▓▓▓

Enlisting chapters to act on your membership recruitment and retention techniques is critical to your organization's success, as doing so helps to drive up membership gains while engaging current members.

"As a national association, it's difficult to make a large organization feel cozy and personal," says Kris Williams, membership marketing manager of the American College of Emergency Physicians (ACEP), Irving, TX. "By working closely with chapters to develop strategies for membership engagement and enrichment at the local chapter level, members can see the value of belonging to both organizations."

With 53 chapters and 27,000 members, the ACEP offers the following tips for managing a chapter membership challenge:

Keep members active and involved:

1. Invite new members to a local meeting and waive their registration fee.
2. Plan orientations for new members at meetings or at their chapter headquarters.
3. Plan special activities for residents in your chapter and charge a small fee.
4. Consider developing a local association or group for residents and possibly subsidizing administrative costs for this group.

Let members see their name in print or be recognized by colleagues:

5. Send welcome letters to new members.
6. Send a new member kit with your welcome letter or direct new members to your website. Include:
   - A list of chapter staff and member contacts.
   - Current committee list and committee enrollment forms.
   - Publication or course catalog, if applicable.
   - Copy of the latest newsletter.
   - An invitation to your next meeting.
   - Calendar of upcoming events.
7. List names of new members in your newsletter or on your website.
8. Ask board members to send a welcoming e-mail.
9. Identify new members at meetings.
10. Thank members in your publications or at your events for their chapter involvement.
11. Announce chapter achievements. Provide copies of such achievements or brochure to ACEP for inclusion in billing statements or new member kits.

Involve chapter leaders in membership retention:

12. Make sure your board includes member issues as a standing item on the agenda. This is particularly important if you do not have a membership committee.
13. Develop a senior advisory group as mentors to new members. Your senior members will appreciate the recognition and your new members will benefit from the contact.

Source: Kris Williams, Membership-Marketing Manager, American College of Emergency Physicians, Irving, TX.
Phone (800) 798-1822 ext. 3128. E-mail: kwilliams@acep.org

Diversify Strategies to Expand Membership

Look for diverse ways to recruit new members via multiple chapters.

Kris Williams, membership marketing manager, the American College of Emergency Physicians (Irving, TX) recommends trying to integrate a combination of strategies to achieve your goal using the following multi-faceted strategies:

❑ **Offer new members free resources and premiums:** Offer a premium for persons who join by a set date to include a discount on an annual meeting if they join on-site; free or discounted courses; or VIP attendance at meetings with leaders in your field.

❑ **Recruit members on-site at annual and chapter meetings:** Many chapters host continuing education meetings. Take advantage of these to recruit members. Target and invite potential members to your next meeting through an e-mail or direct mail invitation. Consider offering a discount on registration fees if the member joins on-site, and train your staff to ask attendees to join to save on their on-site registration.

❑ **Host a new member welcome reception/orientation at your annual meeting:** Make the reception or orientation fun and emphasize the opportunity to get to know your chapter's leaders and colleagues throughout your organization. Provide the attendees with membership benefit information and direct them to your online membership orientation materials. Serve free, light refreshments or lunch, and ask your chapter president to briefly cover the benefits of belonging to your chapter. Consider also hosting a membership booth, but make sure you promote prize drawings and incentives for stopping by, and have strong recruitment leaders in the booth — the person in the booth selling membership is key to membership promotion.

❑ **Host a membership open house with a renowned speaker:** Target specific organizational leaders in your chapter area to present a speech at a membership open house. Make the hours of the open house flexible, if possible. Keep all presentations short and on target so potential members may drop by when they have a moment. Choose a hot topic in your field and ask the speaker to host a discussion forum during the event. Offer free refreshments or food; networking with chapter leaders; overviews of the chapter and benefits; and incentives to join during the open house.

---

34. Recognize Persons With Consecutive Years of Membership ▬▬

What are you doing to recognize those who have reached milestone years of consecutive membership with your organization? Don't let those years of loyalty go unnoticed.

Here are a few examples of what you can do to recognize those reaching milestone years (e.g. five, 10, 20, 30):

- Develop some attractive membership benefits that are exclusive to milestone members who have achieved a specified number of consecutive years with your organization.

- Recognize milestone members on your website, in your annual report and other publications, categorizing them into particular groups (10 years, 20 years).

- Take out a newspaper ad that lists and recognizes your milestone members.

- Create a wall display in a high-traffic area that includes name plates for milestone members.

- Host a once-a-year event for all members at which milestone members are introduced and publicly recognized.

- Coordinate a special ceremony for those who have reached a pinnacle number of years (e.g. 25 years) with your organization, and give them a special gift as a remembrance of the occasion.

35. Reach Out to Your Community's Newcomers ▬▬

Persons new to a community often represent ideal membership prospects. They, too, benefit by making new acquaintances and gaining firsthand exposure to community issues and events.

Do you have a system in place that helps to identify and invite participation from these new residents? Here are a few ways to begin making connections with newcomers:

- Contact your local Welcome Wagon representatives and offer to provide them with mementos for newcomers in exchange for their names and addresses.

- Host an annual newcomer welcome event in which existing members are encouraged to bring someone they

know who is new to the community in the past year.

- Create an outreach committee and assign newcomer identification and recruitment as one of their responsibilities.

- Make regular contacts with organizations and individuals who are the first to come in contact with newcomers — chambers of commerce, realtors, banks, churches and synagogues, to name a few.

- Test targeted advertising in newspapers and other media outlets with messages directed to these new residents: "New to the community? Jumpstart relationships with new friends by joining us!"

36. Form a Committee for Each Member Category ▬▬

Most organizations have more than one membership category or level, each including a different dues and accompanying benefits structure. If you haven't already done so, why not form a committee for each of those member categories made up of members who contribute at that level.

The goal of having member committees at each of these levels has multiple benefits:

1. Any meaningful form of member involvement helps retention efforts.

2. Members' input on the dues structure and accompanying benefits for that category will help to improve your overall membership program and services. Members may come up with some great ideas you may not have

previously considered.

3. Although managing these committees will require time on your part, committee members' involvement and actions will, long term, allow you to accomplish more with their increasing participation.

Develop a committee responsibilities description that spells out expectations. Enlist members for each committee and share a list of the ways in which they can help: evaluating member benefits, identifying activities and networking opportunities for members in that category and more.

Shaping can-do committees for each of your membership categories will, over time, provide for a much more active and vibrant membership structure.

91 Ways to Recruit & Retain More Members

37. Get Members on Board With Facebook Fan Pages ▨▨

Setting up a Facebook fan page for your membership organization is a great way to unify messages to your membership base. The social networking tool lets you send membership updates, event invitations and other information directly to members' Facebook pages and smartphones.

A Facebook fan page can also direct traffic to your website. Not only can members access this page, all

Facebook users can become fans of your nonprofit's page to get updates about your cause, generating more potential membership interest.

For more information on creating Facebook pages to build a presence, engage an audience and spread your message virally, go to www.facebook.com/FacebookPages.

38. In Tough Economy, Be Sure Member Benefits Add Real Value ▨▨

It's common sense to say your member benefits should add real value. But given the continuing economic slump and high rate of unemployment, communicating this value to your members and potential members is imperative, says Arthur Yann, vice president, public relations, the Public Relations Society of America (PRSA), New York, NY.

PRSA is helping members maximize their membership and handle the tough economy with the following efforts:

❑ **Online job center revamp.** A previously static job board was transformed into a popular, interactive resource. They also added a new Ask the Experts feature to complement their Find a Mentor, Content Library, salary information and free résumé posting resources.

❑ **Help with managing budgets.** PRSA is helping people keep their memberships and get more out of them. Recurring special offers include, for example, giving away free chapter or section memberships with the cost of national membership. Members also have the option to pay their membership with quarterly installments. A hardship program to provide assistance with dues for those members who have been with

PRSA for five years or more and find themselves out of work or disabled was also put into place.

❑ **Provision of members-only insurance programs.** Members can now participate in a wide variety of insurance programs, including business and personal insurance, at preferred rates.

❑ **Continuation of free professional development.** Yann says their goal is to hold at least one free webinar per month for members and others in the profession.

❑ **Completion of website overhaul.** New navigation menus and Google-powered search functionality help busy members find relevant information quickly and easily. The new MyPRSA section allows members to create user profiles and contact lists, and indicate preferences that can be used to deliver news and information that appeals to their individual expertise and interests.

Source: Arthur Yann, Vice President, Public Relations, the Public Relations Society of America, New York, NY. Phone (212) 460-1452. E-mail: arthur.yann@prsa.org

---

Professional Networking Site Links You, Members Online

Could your organization's LinkedIn group be considered a member benefit?

According to Arthur Yann, vice president, public relations, at The Public Relations Society of America (New York, NY) this online networking connection can certainly benefit members and staff alike.

"We know our members have specific preferences for when and where they consume news and other information about our organization. LinkedIn (www. linkedin.com) allows us to communicate with a subset of our members in the way they most prefer, so we know our messages are getting through to them," Yann says. "It also gives us a chance to engage them in beneficial two-

way conversations that tell us about their satisfaction levels and other attitudes toward our organization, which we can then collect, analyze and act upon."

Yann says the PRSA gets about 500 requests per month to join their LinkedIn group. Not all of those requests are from PRSA members though, which gives the PRSA an opportunity to encourage them to visit www.prsa.org and learn about some of the other benefits of becoming a PRSA member.

Members have also used LinkedIn to create subgroups that cater to the specific interests and informational needs of their PRSA micro communities, such as districts, chapters and professional interest sections.

---

39. Keep Testing Membership Products and Services

For dues-paying membership organizations, it's important to keep testing existing products and services and trying new ones. Here are products/services strategies to help you assess what works and what does not:

- Start a member advisory group to review products/services and identify new ones.
- Have more costly products/services — those you otherwise would not be able to offer — sponsored by a business to reduce your costs. Be in a position to measure members' perceptions of these more expensive items.
- Segment and target your audience with specific products/services based on each group's needs and characteristics.
- Test particular products/services for new members on their first anniversary to encourage a second year of membership.

40. Sell Your Membership Program in a 30-second Commercial

Create a 30-second, in-person commercial enabling you to speak eloquently about what your organization, in general, and your membership program, in particular.

At the Greater Raleigh Chamber of Commerce (Raleigh, NC), members create a 30-second commercial to efficiently and effectively promote their businesses to fellow members as a form of networking.

Ginger Baxley, annual campaign manager at the chamber, offers steps to create your 30-second informational commercial:

- ❑ Identify yourself by name, job title and nonprofit.
- ❑ Name your nonprofit's two strongest offerings.
- ❑ Express what the best lead for you is and how that information should be delivered to you.
- ❑ Lastly, identify yourself again by name, title and the name of your nonprofit.
- ❑ Ensure that each time you present your 30-second commercial, you do so with enthusiasm and confidence. Be concise with your message and practice several times before delivering it at a networking opportunity.

Source: Ginger Baxley, Annual Campaign Manager, Greater Raleigh Chamber of Commerce, Raleigh, NC.
Phone (919) 664-7052. E-mail: gbaxley@raleighchamber.org.
Website: www.raleighchamber.org

41. Assign Pivotal Roles to Recruit, Retain Members

Satisfied members are the critical component to any thriving membership organization. Assign the following critical positions within your organization to get and keep new members:

New Member Recruitment Chair

The new member recruitment chair is assigned the task of bringing in new members to the organization with help of staff and volunteers. This chairperson will develop a committee designated to promote the organization and bring in an assigned number of members each month. Determine how many members your organization needs each month to thrive and work with the New Member Recruitment Chair to achieve those goals.

Member Retention Chair

This critical role is designed to orchestrate continued efforts of retention within the organization. Working with key staffers, the member retention chair is assigned the task of communicating with existing members and ensuring their ongoing participation within the organization. This chairperson alerts members to new offerings available within the organization and encourages their ongoing participation at all member events. With the assistance of volunteers and staff, this chairperson will combat attrition within your organization.

Member Satisfaction Chair

This chairperson holds the role of ensuring current members are satisfied with what membership offers them. This chairperson should work closely with member satisfaction staff members to survey members about their needs within the organization. The member satisfaction chair will work closely with the new member recruitment chair and member retention chair to identify and implement member benefits that will not only draw new members, but retain them. This chairperson will orchestrate key surveys throughout the year to measure member satisfaction and address any new needs raised via the surveys.

91 Ways to Recruit & Retain More Members

42. Lure Members With Specials

Looking to boost your membership numbers? So are many country clubs across the country. Draw inspiration from these three innovative ways country clubs are attracting first-time members:

- **Offer special limited memberships.** For a membership drive, staff with a New York country club introduced a new membership option. This option served as a temporary, limited-class, membership category that allowed new members to gain access to the country club's full range of facilities and activities without the obligation of regular membership classes. To qualify, persons had to apply as new club members or have been a previous club member for at least one year prior to the date of application. At the end of the temporary membership, they could elect to join the country club.

- **Give them a bargain.** "Get 15 months of membership for the price of 12." This was a membership special launched by a Northeast country club to increase membership sales. Persons who purchased any level of membership for the next year received membership for the remainder of the current calendar year.

- **Give them choices.** To sign up new members and retain existing ones, officials with a New Hampshire country club offered two special options: New members could prepay half of the next year's membership fee right away and play the remaining season free or pay the first half of the next year's membership fee by mid-December and the second half by mid-March, and receive a $200 discount; existing members could pay half of the next year's membership fee by mid-December and half by mid-March and receive a $200 discount or refer a new member and receive pro shop and/or restaurant credit.

43. Offer Opportunities for Members to Recruit Members

The American Industrial Hygiene Association (AIHA) in Fairfax, VA, offers members a simple way to refer a colleague as a potential new member and a chance to win significant prizes: The AIHA Member Get a Member Campaign.

In one-year, the AIHA gained nearly 300 members through the campaign, bringing total membership to more than 10,700, says Kim Bacon, manager-membership and academy relations.

To take part in the effort, current members simply write the name of an individual they feel may be interested in membership with AIHA on their membership application form. Any current member who refers a new potential member this way is entered into a quarterly drawing for a $250 American Express gift card. Each member referred allows another entry into the drawing.

At year end, all members who referred potential members are also eligible to win the grand prize of attending their choice of the AIHA annual conference or the fall conference. The costs of travel expenses, a four-night hotel stay and registration fees to the conference are covered for the winning member — a total package worth up to $1,000.

AIHA's website features the top three reasons for members to recruit other members:

❏ To strengthen the professional community.

❏ To receive an AIHA pin.

❏ To have the opportunity to win prizes.

Bacon says they plan to increase publicity for the recruitment campaign by including more information in newsletters and e-mail communications.

Source: Kim Bacon, Manager-Membership and Academy Relations, American Industrial Hygiene Association, Fairfax, VA. Phone (703) 849-8888. E-mail: kbacon@aiha.org

---

Seven Tips to Encourage Member-to-member Recruitment

Follow these tips from the American Industrial Hygiene Association (AIHA) to enable members to recruit members:

1. Define who is a potential member. Include coworkers, colleagues, professionals looking for career advancement, members of allied associations, nonmembers who attend allied meetings, local college alumni and students.

2. Know and communicate your member benefits. AIHA's Member Get a Member website offers a downloadable membership application and list of benefits for members to access when recruiting others.

3. Show enthusiasm.

4. Send potential members to the website to learn about your organization.

5. Follow up. Recruiting members requires commitment and diligence of follow-up by existing members.

6. Thank potential members with a handwritten note or e-mail note. The more contact a potential member has with an existing member, the more likely he/she is to join.

7. Thank members who work to recruit others, as well. The AIHA website lists names of members who have had significant recruiting success.

ARTICLE DESIGNATION KEY: RECRUITMENT   RETENTION

44. Five Tips for Successful Face-to-face Member Recruitment ▪▪▪

If you ask members to recruit new members, arm them with information to succeed. Share with them these five tips for face-to-face member recruitment:

1. Know the history and future plans of the organization so that you can answer questions the prospective member might have.

2. Share what membership in the organization has done for you.

3. Let the prospect know what you believe the membership will do for him/her.

4. Bring copies of organization publications (e.g., brochures, newsletters, position statements) and copies of any articles about the organization published in the news media.

5. Have an application form with you, and ask the prospective member to fill it out while you are there. Offer to mail or fax it or provide a self-addressed, stamped envelope.

45. Honesty and Frequency Boost Membership Numbers ▪▪▪

Success for one organization started with a 23 percent drop in membership numbers.

"Our success began with finding our true number," Bonnie Grady, currently president/CEO at the Chamber of Commerce of the Mid-Ohio Valley (Parkersburg, WV), says of her prior position at Carroll County Chamber of Commerce (Westminster, MD).

"When I began (at the Carroll County Chamber), "I was told there were 'around 600' active members," Grady says. "What I found was a lot of dead wood on the books: members who had not renewed, were not active and — in some cases — not even in business anymore. We cleaned up the membership records and, when it all shook out, the true number was 463 (23 percent less than 600). At its highest point over the next six years, it would top out at 669," a 44 percent increase over the true number.

To boost membership, Grady and her staff focused on maximizing the number of "touches" each member received by revamping their ambassadors program.

"Each month, ambassadors drew names from the membership list and then reached out to those members by phone, personal letter, e-mail or in person before their next committee meeting," she says. "Ambassadors could also earn points for arranging to meet a new member at a breakfast or luncheon and introducing their new friend to other members, attending chamber events, submitting new member leads and even for picking up the bagels for the monthly chamber orientation program."

Point leaders were named Ambassador of the Month and Ambassador of the Year.

Ultimately, says Grady, success is all about meeting members' needs. "Whether at a chamber meeting or in line at the grocery store, we all tried to develop opportunities to talk with our members, hear their needs and find ways to address those needs."

Source: Bonnie Grady, President/CEO, Chamber of Commerce of the Mid-Ohio Valley, Parkersburg, WV. Phone (304) 422-3588. E-mail: bgrady@movchamber.org

---

Retention Starts Before Day One

During her tenure at a prior Chamber of Commerce, Bonnie Grady, currently president/CEO at the Chamber of Commerce of the Mid-Ohio Valley (Parkersburg, WV), helped increase membership by 44 percent and enjoyed a 96 percent retention rate.

The membership expert says retention is just as important as recruitment.

"The most important thing to remember is that retention starts before day one," she says. "Before you embark on a membership campaign, make that first call or send that first e-mail, you have to know what it is you're selling. Your membership team must understand the value of membership: What are the benefits? How do they work? What does each benefit mean to each member?"

Grady cites the four most critical aspects of recruiting new members — and retaining members — as:

1. **Signaling value** — Educate prospective members on why they should belong; quantify it, if you can.

2. **Offering exceptional customer service**.

3. **Staying on top of disengaged members** – Identify them, talk to them, bring them back in.

4. **Keeping your numbers clean** — Know your true membership numbers.

---

46. Identify Entry-level Options for New Members ▩

After securing new members for your organization, what steps do you take to retain them and make their first year with you something they will want to repeat?

Do you treat these first-year members any differently than you would others?

Beyond expanding your membership base, a more long-term goal should include building a habit of membership. Since it's been proven time and again that it's easier and less costly to retain members than to recruit replacements, it makes sense to develop a plan that will get first-year members to repeat their experience.

These suggestions will convince first-timers to sign on for a second year:

- Add enticing benefits for two-or-more year members: induction into a club with accompanying special invites, reduced prices on organization logo items and other purchases and more.
- Don't make it easy to drop in and out of membership. Structure your program so lapsed members start over again (at the bottom) if they drop out.
- Publicize names of new members and encourage existing members to welcome them.
- Host a yearlong event series to acquaint new members with your organization and with other new members with whom they can build camaraderie.
- Offer incentives for second-year memberships that help establish a habit of renewing.

Your ability to convince first-year members that a second year's membership will be even better contributes to the overall growth of your membership totals over time.

47. Examine the Age-old Question: Retention or Recruitment? ▩ ▩

Every member-based organization has, at one time or another, wondered if resources would be better expended on retaining current members or searching for new ones.

Here, Dave Stevens, managing partner in Stevens and Stevens (Indianapolis, IN), an association marketing and communication firm, sheds light on this important question.

Retention or recruitment: Which is more important to an association's long-term health?

"Absolutely retention. Low retention is a symptom of bigger issues in the association, and if it's not addressed, your organization will be like a leaky bucket. You can keep filling up on the recruitment side, but you will keep losing on the retention side."

If an association had a budget of $100 for both retention and recruitment, how would that money be best divided?

"In terms of marketing alone, I would say up to 70 percent for recruitment and 30 percent for retention. But retention is far more than marketing. In a sense, every service and benefit an association offers furthers (or detracts from) member retention."

Membership departments have great leverage over recruitment activities but little if any control over many factors influencing retention. What is their role in furthering retention?

"Membership departments should be responsible for monitoring retention rates, understanding why rates are what they are and sounding the alarm, if necessary. If they don't have authority to make changes association-wide, they need to focus the attention of leadership on the issue to ensure appropriate action is taken."

Why does recruitment tend to get the bulk of organizational attention and resources?

"In part because recruitment is more fun, more sexy. It is also very tangible; it's easy for membership departments and boards to look at the new member number and be wowed. A related reason is that because low retention rates can make leadership look bad, they are often explained away, when they really shouldn't be."

If an organization has retention problems, how much should it scale back on recruitment?

"You don't want to turn off the tap altogether. You need to keep some sort of presence out there. In most cases you could probably continue what you have been doing, but refrain from starting any new initiatives. When you are closer to industry standards on retention (ASAE lists average retention rates by trade association and individual societies), you can then start placing a greater focus on recruitment again. Neither can be ignored, but retention should always come first."

How can organizations improve their retention rate?

"In the short term, the most important thing is frequent contact with new members, whether through orientation programs, mentor relationships or anything else relevant. But simply contacting them is not enough if your services are not attractive. The longer term driver of retention is identifying and providing the one or two key resources members can't find anywhere else. Ultimately, retention is all about the value proposition an association offers."

Source: Dave Stevens, Managing Partner, Stevens & Stevens, LLC, Indianapolis, IN. Phone (800) 685-1248, ext. 200. E-mail: dave@stevens-stevens.com. Website: www.stevens-stevens.com

48. Top 10 Lists Draw Potential Members

Lists of the top 10 reasons to join are favored tools of member organization recruiters.

Highlighting benefits such as professional development, trade publications and networking opportunities, such lists can be posted on websites, hung on expo booths or included in promotional literature to provide prospective members with tangible answers to the perennial question, "What's in it for me?"

To see how your list compares to others (and maybe snag an idea or two), check out Top 10 lists of these nonprofits (we've abbreviated some elements for space):

Content not available in this edition

Content not available in this edition

Content not available in this edition

91 Ways to Recruit & Retain More Members

49. Let Members Help Write Your Promotional Materials ▪▪▪

Ever get writer's block when it's time to write a recruitment brochure or other promotional material? Look to your members for assistance.

Meet with a handful of dedicated members. Ask why they are committed. List specific reasons for their participation in your organization. Their perceptions will no doubt provide you with the raw material you seek. Their ability to look from the outside in can identify the ways in which your organization is meeting their wants and needs.

Listen carefully to what they say. Their natural responses to your questions may provide key words or phrases that bring new vitality to your marketing pieces.

In addition to providing you with compelling messages, this effort will strengthen your relationship with the persons involved, making them even more committed members.

50. Program Encourages Members to Recruit Members ▪▪▪

When it comes to growing membership, nothing is better than members recruiting members, says Lori Hatcher, senior vice president of membership and marketing at the Urban Land Institute (ULI), Washington, DC. "Members," she says, "are our best salespeople."

The salespeople she refers to come from ULI's Member-Get-a-Member Contest, which uses points and prizes to encourage current members to recruit new ones.

The program has yielded more than 12,000 new members since being started, and though only a relatively small portion of the overall membership participates, the 2,000 to 2,500 members they recruit every year represent a quarter of all new memberships.

The contest runs from one annual convention to the next, with prizes like ULI-published books and a year of free ULI activities are awarded quarterly to maintain interest throughout the year. Top point-getters are also entered into a drawing for the choice of one of five grand prizes (see box, below).

Though the contest is a national program, the institute's local chapters play an important role in promoting it, says Hatcher. This includes pairing the promotion with other incentives like discounted registration at local events for both recruiter and recruit.

Local participation is further encouraged by $1,000 prizes awarded to the two chapters with the highest number and highest percentage of new members.

The institute maintains a running total of member points and current standings on its website, says Hatcher, noting that the highly automated contest is well worth the effort.

"Some of our more active members bring in 10 or more people in a year," she says.

But it isn't just the institute that benefits.

"Members who come in through the contest have a pre-made connection with the organization," Hatcher says. "They have a friend to walk them around and show them how to get the most out of their membership. That's very valuable in and of itself."

Contact: Lori Hatcher, Senior Vice President, Membership & Marketing, ULI-the Urban Land Institute, Washington, D.C. Phone (804) 270-4837. E-mail: Lori.Hatcher@uli.org. Website: http://www.uli.org/JoinULI/MemberGetAMemberContest.aspx

---

Choose Recruitment Prizes That Reflect Your Institution's Values

Planning a member-driven recruitment campaign such as the one offered by Washington, D.C.-based Urban Land Institute (ULI), as detailed above? Be selective in choosing your prizes, since the incentive to win will be a driving force to getting members engaged and involved in this worthwhile effort.

Lori Hatcher, senior vice president of ULI, says she learned the hard way — by offering generic golf shirts as prizes — to select prizes that reflect the values and aims of an organization.

"Using the things people already value about your organization is so much better," Hatcher says about offering prizes that, while worthwhile, are not connected to your cause. "Not only do you get the chance to advertise the products and services you offer, you don't have to worry about ordering merchandise or finding new prizes every year."

The grand prizes that ULI offers through its member-get-a-member contest reflect this focus by centering on resources already available through the ULI. Those prizes include:

- ULI Library, which includes all ULI's printed books and new books for three years.
- Registration, airfare and hotel for ULI domestic or international conference.
- Registration, airfare and hotel for ULI fall or spring meeting.
- Twenty hours of research by ULI's research staff.
- Free, full-page, four-color advertisement in Urban Land Magazine.

ARTICLE DESIGNATION KEY: ▪▪▪ RECRUITMENT ▪▪▪ RETENTION

51. Increase Memberships By Offering a Test Drive ▦

In today's economy, many families are hanging on to their money — tightly. They may not be as willing to shell out funds for a family membership to a favorite museum or zoo or art center, let alone do so for one with which they are not familiar.

Enter the membership test drive.

Imagine It!-The Children's Museum of Atlanta (Atlanta, GA) encourages people to visit the museum by purchasing regular admission tickets. This allows them to check the museum out and see if it's right for their family. If it is, they are able to apply the amount spent on the regular admission tickets to the cost of membership.

The offer is only good on the same day as the paid visit, but can even be taken advantage of after leaving the building. Visitors can simply fax a copy of their tickets and receipt to the museum before the end of business on the day of the visit.

The idea makes everyone involved a winner: Families get to consider whether the organization is a good fit for them at no risk, and the museum has an easy, affordable way to encourage membership.

52. Seven Fresh Ideas to Recruit Members ▦

Membership organizations must stay on task with member recruitment to maintain and build on the membership base. Try these fresh recruitment ideas to bolster your membership base:

1. **Create a new member recruitment competition.** Work with one of your major donors or sponsors to provide a wow prize like an all-expenses-paid trip or big-screen television for the member with the most recruits in a certain time period.

2. **Create an entertaining and informative DVD about your organization** and distribute to potential members in your community.

3. **Partner with another membership organization** in your area to provide a dual membership that will attract new members for both causes.

4. **Offer one-time significant membership discounts** — for example, half price — to attract those who have considered joining for some time.

5. **Offer a membership incentive that hasn't been done in your community.** For example, give gas or grocery gift cards to draw the attention of members, and pass out flyers at your local gas station or grocery store about the membership drive.

6. **Host a dance or local all-inclusive event.** Invite all community members to get a taste of your organization. Give each attendee a gift and information about membership.

7. **Hold a best recruitment idea contest** complete with prizes in which members submit ways to draw newcomers in to your ranks.

53. Woo Corporate Members With Membership Drive Program ▦

In traditional corporate membership programs, a business purchases an organizational membership for employees to use.

That method is fine, except for one point, says Carrie Roberts, development manager at the Omaha Children's Museum (Omaha, NE) — system benefits tend to go mostly to senior executives.

In contrast, Roberts says, her organization's business-based membership drive program focuses on all employees.

"We partner with area businesses to offer membership drives that cater to the needs of their employees," Roberts says. "Whether we set up an on-site booth or just provide an electronic campaign, we give people the chance to join our institution at a rate that is reduced to start with and often further subsidized by their employer."

The program is a classic win-win situation, says Roberts. Participating businesses receive an attractive employee benefit to highlight in recruiting efforts, and the museum receives a steady stream of new members. A typical drive, lasting a few days to several weeks, can yield anywhere from a handful of members in small businesses, to more than 100.

Roberts says most of the museum's corporate partners prefer electronic campaigns that require fewer human resources than non-online drives. In e-campaigns, museum staff play a largely advisory role, and a company liaison — supplied with drive guidelines, payment options and reproducible or e-mailable PDFs of membership brochures and current exhibits — oversees most day-to-day details.

Roberts says the program, entering its second year and still developing, generates around three membership drives a month.

Source: Carrie Roberts, Development Manager, Omaha Children's Museum, Omaha, NE. Phone (402) 342-6164, ext. 423. E-mail: croberts@ocm.org

54. Drive Yields $110,000, Draws 281 New Members ▨

Three days, almost 300 volunteers, 281 new members and $110,000 in dues equal one successful membership drive, but you might not guess the most important ingredient of all: rock and roll.

"The Rock the Chamber theme created immense buzz in the business community," says Gayle Anderson, president and CEO of the Greater Winston-Salem Chamber of Commerce (Winston-Salem, NC). "I can't tell you how many people said to me, 'I've got to do this just to see what the heck is going on.'"

The interest generated around the peer-to-peer calling campaign was no accident. Chamber officials created a fictitious rock band and worked hard to promote it, with Anderson dressing in leather, carrying a guitar, and giving interviews as her rock superstar alter ego, Hurricane Anderson.

The theme was part of an overall strategy created in consultation with Your Chamber Connection, a Fort Worth, TX-based consultancy emphasizing fast-paced, high-energy events.

But while the drive was lighthearted fun for volunteers, it was careful planning and logistics for organizers. Twelve campaign captains were recruited from chamber members and commissioned to recruit five separate teams of volunteers. Each of the captains' teams was then assigned responsibility for one of the drive's five calling sessions.

In each two-and-a-half-hour session, volunteers were given a thorough orientation on how a chamber benefits businesses and how it can be sold to prospective members. The actual calling was done in a festive atmosphere of energizing music and cheering for each new membership.

Since the completion of the campaign, officials at many chambers of commerce have contacted Anderson. Her advice is always the same: Be willing to go all in or don't do it at all. She explains that the success of Rock the Chamber required her entire staff of 18 for a full week, with many additional hours beyond that.

She also advises trusting consultants. "If you are going to hire them in the first place, do exactly what they say," she says. "They have done this many times and know how to make it work, so just trust the advice they give you."

Source: Gayle Anderson, President and CEO, The Greater Winston-Salem Chamber of Commerce, Winston-Salem, NC.
Phone (336) 728-9200. E-mail: anderson@winstonsalem.com

55. Give Members a Reason to Belong ▨ ▨

Persons looking for motivation to join or renew their membership in the Mooresville-South Iredell Chamber of Commerce (Mooresville, NC) don't have to look far. The chamber's website posts 10 reasons why membership with the chamber is so important:

1. **New business contacts:** Networking and new business contacts help your business grow. With nearly 1,100 members representing thousands of area employees, the chamber speaks with a strong voice for our business community.
2. **Credibility:** Credibility to make a statement that you are committed to the future of Iredell County.
3. **Leadership development:** Learning opportunities/ professional development to help you run a smarter, more profitable business.
4. **Community commitment:** Promote the community to help residents enjoy greater opportunities.
5. **Referrals:** Referrals and sales opportunities to deliver return on your investment.
6. **Publicity and exposure:** Publicity and heightened name recognition so customers know who you are.
7. **Marketing and advertising:** Targeted and affordable advertising to help your business effectively grow on any budget.
8. **A healthy local environment:** Create a strong local economy to keep our business momentum moving forward.
9. **A voice in the government:** The chamber is your representative on the local, regional, state and national level. Your voice is heard on vital regulatory, legislative and educational issues affecting your business.
10. **Activities:** Getting involved in the many activities the chamber has to offer leads to valuable relationships and gratification in serving the community.

Source: Karen Shore, President/CEO, Mooresville-South Iredell North Carolina Chamber of Commerce, Mooresville, NC.
Phone (704) 664-3898. E-mail: kas@mooresvillenc.org

56. Offer Multi-year Membership as a Retention Tool ▬

To retain a larger percentage of members from year to year, consider offering multiple-year membership specials from time to time.

Although some organizations make multiple-year memberships a standard option, offering this alternative from time to time can grab members' attention and make it a more attractive consideration.

Here are three examples of multiple-year membership options you may wish to promote as a special limited-time offer:

1. **Sliding-scale option** — Charge your regular rate for year one with a decreasing membership amount for year two and even less for year three.

2. **Two-for-one option** — Anyone who purchases a three-year membership receives an additional one-year membership for the individual (or business) of their choice. Additional membership is only good for a new member.

3. **Multi-year premiums option** — Those who purchase multiple year memberships receive exclusive premiums.

57. How to Prepare and Draft a Membership Marketing Plan ▬

Membership organizations focus on few things more fervently than acquiring new members. And few things are more central to this than creating an effective membership marketing plan.

Here, Mark Levin, president of the business management consulting agency, BAI Inc. (Columbia, MD) and executive vice president of the Chain Link Fence Manufacturers Institute (Columbia, MD), discusses the ins and outs of this important recruiting tool.

What are the questions that need to be answered before developing a membership marketing plan?

"You need to know where the plan ranks among your association's priorities. If you don't have the full support of staff and volunteer leadership, you shouldn't undertake a plan. You also need to clearly define how you will measure success. Take, for example, a goal of increasing membership by 10 percent. Will you take any members you can get, or do you want to target specific demographics? Is retention important to you, or do you not care how many people you lose as long as the total grows by 10 percent? Differing answers to these questions can lead to sharply differing plans, even though they share the same ultimate goal."

> *"Any plan is based on assumptions — assumptions about what the economy will do, what the industry will do, what the government will do."*

What are some of the key elements of a well-crafted marketing plan?

"The presentation document should include the central objective, measurement criteria, key initiatives, a summary of current ongoing initiatives, concrete membership goals, and I recommend at least one new initiative planned for each key area of the plan. The membership department should also have the details of implementation worked out internally, though those won't be shared as widely."

Are there elements of a membership plan that are often overlooked?

"Any plan is based on assumptions — assumptions about what the economy will do, what the industry will do, what the government will do. These assumptions should be explicit and included in the plan so that it can be adjusted if those conditions change and evolve."

What sort of time frame should a membership marketing plan address?

"Any plan of any significant detail over two years long is difficult to stick to because the membership environment changes so quickly. Anticipating conditions more than two years out is guesswork as much as anything."

Are there mistakes organizations often make in producing a marketing plan?

"Many plans are very weak on prioritization. Everybody can generate numbers and goals, but those goals have to be prioritized to determine the order in which to expend resources. You have to be able to say which parts of the plan you have to have, and which parts you would only like to have. This tells you what could be cut if needed, because something always has to be cut in the end."

You have a membership marketing plan in hand; what should you do to most effectively implement it?

"You should make sure that you are regularly adjusting it, as the assumptions it was based on change. When people fixate on one number or one approach and fail to take into account changes in the environment, they tend to assume their plan was just wrong from the beginning. But that's often not the case. You might have created the right plan for the right time, but the times changed underneath you."

Source: Mark Levin, President, BAI Incorporated and Executive Vice President, Chain Link Fence Manufacturers Institute, Columbia, MD. Phone (301) 596-2584. E-mail: Mlevin0986@aol.com

58. Proven Recruitment Strategies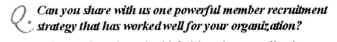

Q. Can you share with us one powerful member recruitment strategy that has worked well for your organization?

"Up-to-date tools and good, old-fashioned personalization are the best recruitment strategies for our museum. Make the website wonderful. Showcase what you do and make it easy to join, plus keep the personal touch where possible. Sign and personalize your membership letters, keep good notes and make sure you answer the phone."

— *Kirsten Alexander, Senior Membership Manager, Historic New England (Boston, MA)*

"Develop strategic alliances. Most nonprofits focus their energy on recruiting one or two members at a time, but in reality, they need to grow their organizations by hundreds. When an organization forms strategic alliances with other organizations and comes up with a mutually beneficial strategy, both organizations grow and are committed to success."

— *Rosanna Imbriano, Director, The Center for Italian and Italian-American Culture (Cedar Grove, NJ)*

"Our Open Your Address Book campaign, asking members to send in contact information of friends and colleagues —

each name provided by a member enters that member into a drawing for an iPad, iTouch and cash prizes. Over 1,000 names were generated from the campaign, and many have joined the association and registered for upcoming conferences."

— *Megan D'Ariano, Membership Coordinator, Association Headquarters (Mount Laurel, NJ)*

"My most successful strategy was to diminish the stress felt by potential members by assigning a group of four to five hosts or hostesses to take responsibility for each guest who attends a social event for the first time. The hosts/hostesses introduce them to as many people as possible and then pass them on to another host/hostess. It usually takes two to three social visits for a person to join."

— *Ellen Lytle, former Director, Medici Center (Atlanta, GA)*

"Allow everybody to shine by pinpointing their talents and encouraging them to share their creativity. This allows them to have a voice, and also, don't we all want to feel worthy and loved?"

— *Terry Grahl, Founder and President, Enchanted Makeovers (Taylor, MI)*

59. Two Initiatives Grow Museum's Membership by 30 Percent

Over the past three years, staff and supporters of the Family Museum (Bettendorf, IA) have seen new memberships grow, thanks to implementation of two initiatives:

Initiative 1: Offering Discounts for Timely Renewals

Evaluating membership renewal habits, Jeff Reiter, business development manager, found that members who were due to renew in the summer months often let memberships lapse. Reiter initiated the effort offering summer membership renewals the opportunity to renew by June 1 and receive a $10 discount on the membership fee. This effort helped to nearly double the number of memberships for summertime renewals over years past, and allowed the museum to bank the membership fees before the end of its fiscal year in July.

Initiative 2: Partnering With Other Member-based Organizations

The second highly successful initiative began in 2004 when the museum staff offered a collaborative membership with two other family-oriented facilities in the Quad Cities area. Through Triple Membership, members can purchase an annual membership to the Family Museum, Putnam Museum and Imax Theatre, and the Niabi Zoo.

Reiter says collaborating was a natural fit for the three organizations, as they share some common trustees and board members who suggested the combined effort. "From a

marketing perspective," Reiter says, "the three organizations also realized they all share an audience in the community."

Membership benefits for this category include allowing two adults and all children under age 18 in the same household to receive membership benefits at the Family Museum, Putnam Museum and Niabi Zoo. This level includes all basic member benefits at each facility, plus reciprocal admission to more than 275 science and technology centers and reciprocity to more than 50 zoos — a package valued at $225.

The combined annual fee for the membership was set at $160 and was met with tremendous response by members, he says. But officials with the three organizations realized that at that price point, they were not redeeming the added revenue desired. So, with some trepidation, they increased the price to $190. The membership audience did not balk at the increased price and continued to select Triple Membership that now makes up nearly 30 percent of the Family Museum's membership base.

"These two initiatives allowed us to grow from 914 memberships, an all-time low, to 1,308 memberships which is close to an all-time high," says Reiter. "We grew roughly 30 percent of our membership base."

Source: Jeff Reiter, Business Development Manager, Family Museum, Bettendorf, IA. Phone (563) 334-4106. E-mail: jreiter@bettendorf.org

60. Recruitment Ideas

Sometimes even the most obvious member recruitment ideas get overlooked. Consider these reliable techniques:

1. Offer a percentage discount for first-year members.

2. Encourage members to refer prospects by offering a small prize to those who provide a set number of names.

3. When calling on prospective members, send volunteers out in pairs. It's more impressive, and solicitors can support each other during the presentation.

4. Provide a trial membership allowing persons to attend events or meetings at no cost for a set time period.

5. Assign a veteran member to sponsor a potential member both during and after the application process.

61. Active Membership Equals Strong Retention Rates

The San Francisco Bicycle Coalition (SFBC) of San Francisco, CA, has grown from 116 members in 1992 to more than 10,000 members today, thanks to a staff that excels at both attracting new members and retaining existing ones.

"Because we encourage our members to also volunteer within our organization, our members have a high level of engagement, which equals a high level of retention," says Kate McCarthy, membership and volunteer director of SFBC.

Ways SFBC continues to grow membership while keeping members active include:

✓ **Streetside campaigns** — SFBC hosts ongoing streetside campaigns throughout the year where members literally line the streets at their self-made service stations to assist bicyclists during their commutes. Member volunteers pump air into bike tires and offer bike lights and bells, commuter totes, coffee and snacks for riders. The streetside service model is in full force on Bike to Work Day. The SFBC offers 27 Energizer Station locations for biking commuters with the help of 300 member volunteers and, for the past two years, has netted about 700 annual memberships.

✓ **Barter memberships** — SFBC offers memberships via a barter arrangement to persons who are highly active volunteers or cannot afford a standard membership. Barter memberships require the member to serve 10 volunteer hours in exchange for membership payment. McCarthy says barter members who volunteer 10 or more hours tend to be more dedicated to the mission and retention in this group remains high. In the past year, 125 household barter memberships were secured. Barter members sign a barter membership agreement and receive membership cards after serving the minimum volunteer requirement. "Ten hours is a significant contribution and we feel this is a nice number to allow us to build a strong relationship with that member," says McCarthy.

✓ **One-to-one member outreach** — While one-to-one member outreach isn't a new idea, the way SFBC handles it is. Currently, the SFBC houses 500 trained member-volunteers who effectively recruit other members via outreach efforts. Training member-volunteers to conduct outreach gives members the knowledge to speak in an educated fashion about the mission of the organization. Training entails a one-hour workshop where the organization's mission and goals are taught to members who then go on to share that message in the community.

Source: Kate McCarthy, Membership and Volunteer Director, San Francisco Bicycle Coalition, San Francisco, CA. Phone (415) 431-2453 ext. 303. E-mail: Kate@sfbike.org

Content not available in this edition

62. Seek to Recruit Face-to-face ▓▓

While you have a wealth of recruitment methods at your disposal — phone, personal correspondence, website, advertising and more — no technique is as effective as a face-to-face, one-on-one call.

Face-to-face recruitment:
- Conveys greatest urgency.
- Best eliminates possible objections.

- Demonstrates personalized need for an individual's participation.
- Provides for an immediate response.

While you may employ a number of recruitment methods, remember there's no substitute for the personal approach.

63. Three Easy Ways to Gain New Members ▓▓

Members are the lifeblood of every membership-based organization.

Try these three ways to inject new blood into your organization and reinvigorate your membership program:

1. Raffle a free membership to community members.
2. Remind members to bring friends to the next event or meeting. Have membership packets handy at the meeting, along with persons able and willing to answer any questions and host a drawing for free membership — all new arrivals eligible.
3. Ask members for names of friends and colleagues who would benefit from membership. Send this group a personal invitation to attend your next special event.

64. Attract Current and Prospective Members With a Trunk Show ▓▓ ▓▓

Looking for a new event to bring current and prospective members to your door?

Host a trunk show, in which vendors bring their merchandise directly to your invited guests.

Since 2007, The Morikami Museum & Japanese Gardens (Delray Beach, FL) has hosted nearly a dozen trunk shows. The special merchandise sales are free and open to members and nonmembers alike, with an average of 25 to 50 members attending.

Sallie Chisholm, museum store manager, says she got the idea to regularly host trunk shows after the museum hosted a designer trunk show for an advancement fundraiser: "I thought, 'let's try organizing some more trunk shows using vendors from whom we normally purchase merchandise and give them a chance to sell more products and share the profits.'"

While vendors are not charged to participate in trunk shows, the museum receives a pre-negotiated percentage of each sale made during the shows, says Chisholm, who adds that they typically purchase some items to complement the museum store's existing inventory.

Jewelry trunk shows are proving the most popular, she says, adding that they are considering combining more than one type of vendor to increase the shows' appeal.

The museum has also hosted trunk shows featuring the craft of Temari balls and vintage silk haori (jackets) and kimonos from Japan.

To publicize the trunk shows, they send out an e-mail blast and hand out fliers in the store a few weeks in advance. In some instances, they provide information regarding the trunk shows to their public relations firm so press releases can be sent.

Chisholm says they plan to create a banner that will

Show Doubles as Member Recruitment Effort

Since trunk shows offered by The Morikami Museum & Japanese Gardens (Delray Beach, FL) are open to the public as well as members, staff use these events as member recruitment opportunities.

Nonmembers are encouraged to sign up for membership during the trunk show by being offered a discount on their purchases.

The current discount is 20 percent off their purchase on the day they sign up for membership. Signage is posted in the museum store during the event that says:

"Not a member yet? Ask how to receive 20% off your purchases in the Museum Store for today only!"

hang in the museum's main entrance emblazoned with a generic message, such as "Trunk show this Saturday at Morikami Museum store." The banner will also include the organization's website.

Museum store staff usually helps with trunk show setup and breakdown as needed. Vendors can request 6- or 8-foot tables to display their products, which include fabric table skirts and velvet toppers which were made by staff members. In addition, vendors may use a large mirror and floor easel provided by the museum.

For member organizations considering hosting a trunk show, Chisholm recommends scheduling your shows on days when you are expecting high traffic.

Source: Sallie Chisholm, Museum Store Manager, The Morikami Museum & Japanese Gardens, Delray Beach, FL. Phone (561) 495-0233, ext. 212. E-mail: SChishol@pbcgov.org

65. Day Trips Offer Member-friendly, Loyalty-building Experiences

Looking for a way to connect with members? Offer day-long excursions to area attractions.

The Newark Museum (Newark, NJ) hosts some two dozen day trips every year, which are popular with members, says Merle Lomrantz, director of member travel services.

"The trips are not inexpensive, but people really feel they are getting a great value," says Lomrantz. "They don't have to worry about where to park, where to eat lunch, how to get from place to place. They just have to show up — and they love it."

Lomrantz discusses some details of running a day-trip program.

What does a typical day trip look like?

"Most tours feature two main activities. We will leave the museum at 8 a.m. and start with a private, before-hours tour of a museum followed by a relaxed lunch at an outstanding restaurant. After lunch, we follow up with a related workshop, lecture or tour. Most day trips end at 6 p.m."

What kind of attractions go into a good day trip program?

"Everything we do is educational, so we love trips that tie into exhibitions showing at our museum. Because of the diversity of this area, we also run trips exploring, for example, African American, Latino, Jewish and Muslim cultural traditions. In everything we do we want to be timely and cutting edge. We want to be where everyone wants to go."

Are some kinds of trips reliably more popular than others?

"Yes. Blockbuster exhibitions at other museums are always popular. Tours of historic houses are also great. Any interesting place that people wouldn't otherwise have access to or wouldn't want to drive to has potential."

Are there activities or destinations you avoid?

"We don't like to go anywhere our members won't feel special, so we try to avoid public festivals or shows. If we are visiting an exhibition at another institution we always arrange a private tour led by a curator or docent, preferably before or after hours."

Where do you come up with themes for your tours?

"I read a lot of regional publications like *New York Magazine, New Jersey Monthly* and the *New York Times,* looking for ideas. I also ask tour members for suggestions as we're riding the bus."

Who is a typical day-trip participant?

"Different programs attract different demographics, but our typical participant is an empty nester in his or her 50s or 60s, a cultural consumer who wants to go to top museums, have fabulous lunches and learn as much as possible. We have experimented with family programs, but by the time everyone is paid for, the trip isn't really cost effective. Time and money are the two necessities for day-trippers, and that usually suggests retirees."

What does a day-trip program do for the museum?

"We call it a friendraiser. The trips promote interest in and affiliation with the museum, and in many cases the experience prompts people to increase their level of membership. Indirectly, they can also help generate bequests and other gifts."

Source: Merle Lomrantz, Director of Member Travel Services, Newark Museum, Newark, NJ. Phone (973) 596-6643. E-mail: mlomrantz@newarkmuseum.org

---

Practical Tips for Creating, Operating Day-trip Program

Is a day-trip program right for your member-based organization?

Merle Lomrantz, director of member travel services at the Newark Museum (Newark, NJ), which regularly offers day-trip options to members, shares some insight into the nuts-and-bolts administration of such a program:

- ❑ **Logistical details**. Meals, bus service, tour guides and event site arrangements are just some of the details that can require contracts, negotiations and documentation, says Lomrantz. One important skill is estimating the minimum, maximum and likely number of attendees.

- ❑ **Group size**. Fifty people is the upper limit for a comfortable tour, says Lomrantz. "Busses can hold 55, but you need a little room for people to spread out. More than that isn't enjoyable."

- ❑ **Eligibility**. Day trips used to be open to the public, but eight years ago, museum officials decided to restrict participation to members. "There was some concern that it might detract from the tours, but just the opposite happened — it led to an increase in membership," says Lomrantz.

- ❑ **Lead time**. Lomrantz says she likes to finalize tours six to nine months in advance. "Tours can sell out three to four months in advance, depending on programming, and all arrangements should be formalized before advertising the trip."

- ❑ **Travel time**. Three hours one way is the longest Lomrantz will consider traveling on a day trip. She tries to keep most trips under 90 minutes one way.

- ❑ **Market research**. Consulting your constituency to determine their level of interest and price point is the first step in starting a day trip program, says Lomrantz. "Planning a tour takes a lot of work, so you really need to test your market to make sure the demand is there to support it."

ARTICLE DESIGNATION KEY: ▊ RECRUITMENT ▊ RETENTION

66. Encourage Members to Renew Early With Incentives

Create a program to provide members with worthwhile incentives for early renewal.

Staff with the Greater Brandon Chamber of Commerce (Brandon, FL) started their renewal rewards program in 2006 to reward members who paid dues prior to their anniversary date, says Janet Noah, director, member services.

The program began after an area newspaper and chamber member offered $100 vouchers good toward any new ad purchased in any of its publications for chamber members who renewed early.

The rewards program revolves around chamber members donating prizes as incentive to renew before the anniversary date, says Noah. Initially, she reached out to a variety of members to see if they would be interested in participating in this program. Once a few members came on board, other members began to inquire about participating.

Rewards range from a mail center coupon, free meal, free ads in chamber and other publications and free flyer placements, as well as the chance to win member-donated prizes. Members who donate prizes are listed in the cham-ber's monthly newsletter and on its website.

Current members are reminded about the renewal rewards in two ways, a member renewal page on the chamber's website and on the invoices they receive prior to their renewal date. The chamber is not currently tracking how many members renewed early because of this program.

When developing a renewal rewards program, Noah advises, start simply. Consider sending a mass mailing to tell members about the program and ask them to donate prizes. While prizes need not be extravagant, strive to gather a variety of prizes to appeal to more of your members.

Once you have the donated prizes in place, look for ways to publicize this program to members and get them excited about the possibility of winning rewards. Allow members to renew online, by mail, at events and in person at your office.

Finally, remember to market this prize incentive to people considering becoming members of your organization.

Source: Janet Noah, Director, Member Services, The Greater Brandon Chamber of Commerce, Brandon, FL. Phone (813) 689-1221. E-mail: jnoah@brandonchamber.com

67. Building Auxiliary Membership One Brochure at a Time

The Emerson Hospital Auxiliary (Concord, MA) is always looking to add quality members to its group. Helping the auxiliary do so is a detailed, full-color membership brochure.

The four-panel brochure is printed on heavy stock and features these categories:

- Making a Difference — describes six ways members' efforts assist the organization.
- Who We Are — shares the auxiliary's history.
- What We Do — provides greater detail about the organization and how it assists the hospital.
- Becoming a Member — this tear-away panel acts as a member registration form.
- Testimonials — existing members share why they belong to the auxiliary, reassuring potential members that becoming a member is a wise move.
- Enjoy the Benefits of Membership — details the rewards that people receive when they become a member with your organization.

Source: Karen McCarthy, Vice President of Membership, Emerson Hospital Auxiliary, Concord, MA. Phone (978) 287-3019.

This detailed brochure helps recruit members to the Emerson Hospital Auxiliary (Concord, MA).

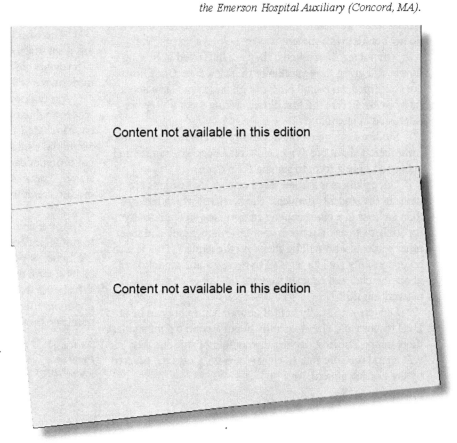

Content not available in this edition

Content not available in this edition

68. Involve Members in Decisions ▮▮▮

If you're gearing up for a capital campaign, revamping your website or testing new collaterals, make sure to get members involved in the process. Asking their opinion takes little time and can garner useful feedback. Doing so also makes them feel as if they are making a positive contribution to the organization — one that's not monetary — and fosters good will.

69. Dinner Club Engages Current and Prospective Members ▮▮▮

Looking to engage prospective members? Create a dinner club that allows current members to serve as hosts while encouraging social interaction and networking.

Staff with the Lehigh University Alumni Association (Bethlehem, PA) began The Student & Alumni Dinner Club in October 2007, says Chad Davis, associate director of student and young alumni programs.

The dinner club's purpose is simple, Davis says: "Lehigh alumni hosting students at their homes for a meal, conversation and an evening of fun. It gives current students the opportunity to interact with alumni in a casual and unusual environment."

The dinner club was formed after the alumni association's former executive director attended a conference and spoke with other schools that had successfully used a similar program.

"It is our goal to have at least 20 dinners hosted every year, while hopefully increasing the number of first-time hosts every semester," says Davis.

Planning begins with staff designating two to three weeks on the academic calendar for possible dinner dates that do not conflict with student breaks, holidays, exams, etc.

Alumni are then asked if they are interested in hosting a dinner and given the opportunity to pick a date. Once hosts are confirmed, an e-mail is sent to all undergraduates about three weeks before the first dinner, asking them if they are interested in attending.

Students can go on the university's website to view more information about the dinner club, read host biographies and submit an online form to sign up for a dinner.

Once dinners are filled, three orientation sessions are held for the student attendees. The sessions, which last less than an hour in a classroom on campus, are an opportunity for students to ask questions about the dinner club and meet other students who will be attending the dinners. This is also an opportunity for alumni staff to review some guidelines about the club and educate students on dinner etiquette and networking skills.

Dinners are usually held at alumni homes but can be at local restaurants. They generally begin around 6 p.m. and last three hours. The host decides the number of students who will attend (usually four to eight students). Costs are covered by the hosting alumni.

Dinner Club Benefits All Involved

Chad Davis, associate director of student and young alumni programs, Lehigh University Alumni Association (Bethlehem, PA), shares three ways the association's dinner club benefits those involved:

✓ "First, the dinners connect students with alumni and the alumni association in a very casual and informal way.

✓ "Second, they connect alumni with students and the university.

✓ "Third, they connect students with each other. The program allows students to expand their connections and interact with students with whom they might not normally sit down and have a meal. However, I think the true sign of success will be several years from now, when we have students who participated in the program asking to host dinners as alumni."

"There isn't a formal structure to the night, and we really just want students and alumni to talk and interact," says Davis. "The dinner club is alcohol-free, and alumni and students are made aware of this policy prior to participating in the program."

Alumni hosts receive a thank-you gift from student attendees, which is provided by the alumni association. "Gifts have included a porcelain plate with a picture of the Alumni Memorial Building and a copy of The Little Brown Box, a collection of cards that detail some of Lehigh's traditions and stories," says Davis. In addition, alumni can also receive gift-in-kind credit from the university for their participation in the program.

Any member organization could modify the dinner club to suit their needs. Members could host prospective members for dinner or perhaps even create a new members dinner club so long-term members can get to know the newest members. Whichever format a membership organization chooses, it is important to set clear guidelines and expectations and communicate these frequently with all participants.

Source: Chad Davis, Associate Director of Student and Young Alumni Programs, Lehigh University Alumni Association, Bethlehem, PA. Phone (610) 758-3137. E-mail: chad.davis@lehigh.edu

70. Hold a Membership Drive ▩

Seek the help of staff and members to host a well-planned membership drive. Here are steps for doing so:

Prepare for the Drive

- ❑ Set a goal. Determine how many new members you need to sign to meet your recruitment needs.
- ❑ Involve staff in planning an open house/recruitment event. Train them on fielding membership inquiries and proactively recruiting members. Offer incentives for working at the open house and signing on new members.
- ❑ Create a fact sheet that details membership and its benefits. Print application on back to make enrollment easy.
- ❑ Create a Q&A section on your website where potential members can get answers about membership.
- ❑ Create a display or Microsoft PowerPoint presentation that shows your membership events, service opportunities and the benefits of membership.
- ❑ Create a giveaway that entices membership by a predetermined date.
- ❑ Send invitations to potential and current members. Ask members and staff to spread the word and invite friends who are strong membership candidates.
- ❑ Heavily advertise the event and draw in likely members with a gift or membership discount for attending.

Hold an Open House

- ❑ Set up information tables where staff can field questions from attendees.
- ❑ Have guests sign in with mailing address, e-mail and other contact info.
- ❑ Have staff mingle to boost conversation with potential members.

Follow Up

- ❑ Perhaps the single most important key of a successful membership drive is the follow-up. Compare the list of attendees to those who signed on to become members.
- ❑ Have staff and member volunteers call new members to welcome them and invite them to events. For attendees who did not join, call and thank them for attending, ask if they have questions and offer a reduced membership rate.
- ❑ Follow up with new and potential members again in three to six months.

71. Buddies Mentor New Members ▩

The Meeting Professionals International-Wisconsin Chapter (Madison, WI), has developed a mentoring program designed to create teams that will initiate new members to their program.

"The goal of the mentor program is to ensure all chapter members receive the support and professional guidance they require," says Susan Kainz, vice president of membership. "There is a wealth of experience and knowledge in our chapter, and there is no greater satisfaction than being able share it with other meeting professionals."

The 370-member chapter enlisted members who have expertise as meeting professionals to support new members on a one-on-one basis. At a recent chapter meeting, 30 new members and buddies were partnered, says Kainz.

When new persons join, the membership committee sends someone to welcome them to the organization. New members are asked if they would like a buddy to help them stay informed about the organization, stay connected with other members, share rides or sit with at meetings.

The buddy mentoring system can also lead to assisting the new member with preparing for the Certified Meeting Professional test.

Kainz offers three tips to successfully matching new members with buddies:

1. **Location:** Chapter members who live in the same city can share rides to member events and connect to utilize professional resources.

2. **Years of experience:** They seek to match members based on years of experience, realizing that a new member who has many years of experience in the industry has different needs than someone just entering the profession.

3. **Students:** These new members are paired with experienced members who have gone through the hospitality programs and the three technical schools in Wisconsin. Members guide students on how to prepare for a career in the meeting planning industry.

Source: Susan Kainz, Vice President of Membership for Meeting Professionals International-Wisconsin and Director of Sales and Marketing of The Delafield Hotel, Madison, WI.
Phone (608) 204-9816. E-mail: susank@thedelafieldhotel.com

72. Three Solid Steps to Member Recruitment

New members are essential to any membership organization. Try these tips to gain new recruits and maintain and grow your membership levels:

1. Contact businesses not represented within your membership and set up a time to present details about your organization to a group of their employees. Additionally, send personal invitations to notables in your community who could bring a high profile to your organization. Once they join your organization, ask them to refer colleagues and business contacts to join in a member-get-a-member campaign.

2. Invite potential members to attend an upcoming event with no strings attached. Follow all invitations with a personal call or e-mail reminder. Once they participate in an event, persons are more likely to become members. Make a follow-up call after a potential member has attended an event to personally ask them to join.

3. Join forces with another organization aligned with the goals of your group to offer a dual membership at a discounted price. Co-host an event to feature the positive aspects of each organization and design a presentation that highlights how joining both groups is a benefit to members beyond the discounted membership cost.

73. Offer Rookie Tours for New Members

Offering new members a tour of your facility not only engages new members, it brings them to a comfort level with your organization, which allows them to utilize their membership to the fullest.

Phoenix Art Museum (Phoenix, AZ) has brought about the concept of new member tours. With the onset of the economic downturn, the museum began offering the new member tours, also known as Rookie Tours, as an inexpensive way to retain new members.

Offered monthly, the tours welcome members who joined in the last four weeks, with as many as 25 spaces available for each tour.

Tammy Stewart, membership and visitor services manager, shares more details about the popular new member tours:

✓ A personal note in welcome packets invites new members to the tour. Tours are mentioned in the welcome phone call received by each new member. They also receive a brief e-mail reminder about the event and, once their tour is complete they receive a personal thank-you note — all steps to help ensure that the member participates in a tour and to goodwill toward the organization is fostered.

✓ Staff members, not always curators, lead the tours, offering behind-the-scenes thoughts, ideas and styles. Each participating staff member creates a tour that is unique and individualized by his/her perception of the museum. For example, the director of education created a tour that served two purposes: to offer a personally guided tour of the museum for new members, and to use the group of 20 or so attendees as a focus group with whom she could share her new ideas and obtain feedback.

✓ Each tour has a specific topic or theme. For example, one tour features tips on observing art, while another notes the unique architecture throughout the museum.

✓ The tours are orchestrated so that the guide leads the new members to many parts of the museum, causing them to become acquainted and familiar with all the nuances of the organization.

✓ Those who successfully complete the tour receive a parting gift, such as a coffee mug with the museum's logo on it.

✓ Museum staffers select a night for the tour when other events are taking place — such as a film showing or lecture — so new members experience other events available with their new membership. Additionally, the tour night coincides with an evening when the museum's café is open for dinner, where members receive a discount, another benefit that members can experience when the tour is complete.

✓ Upon completion of the six-month pilot program, Tammy Stewart, membership and visitor services manager, will determine the effects the tours have had on new member retention.

"Our rookie tours have given our members an opportunity to learn more about their museum in an informal environment and allow staff to build relationships with our newest members," says Stewart. "Combined with no direct costs and little staff time compared to other member events, this addition to our program has been a success. We hope to see a positive impact on new member retention."

Source: Tammy Stewart, Membership and Visitor Services Manager, Phoenix Art Museum, Phoenix, AZ. Phone (602) 257-2124. E-mail: Tammy.Stewart@phxart.org. Website: www.phxart.org

91 Ways to Recruit & Retain More Members

74. Are You Making a Sufficient Number of Awards?

There's nothing like a deserved award to warm the hearts of those associated with your nonprofit or association.

While it's important to make awards for legitimate reasons, there's no denying they also serve to cultivate relationships.

Based on your type of organization and your mission, are there awards you could be making to worthy recipients? Some examples of award recipients include:

❑ Members, board members and/or volunteers.
❑ Chapter leaders.
❑ Youth or senior citizens.
❑ Families.
❑ Minorities.
❑ Other organizations or associations.
❑ Businesses and corporations.
❑ Persons who exemplify your mission.

To celebrate your member-based organization and the people who make all you do possible, consider giving awards based on:

❑ Service to your organization.
❑ Service to the community, region, state or nation.
❑ Years of service.
❑ An act of heroism.

Where do awards opportunities exist for your organization? Assemble your awards committee and explore the possibilities.

75. 11 Member Recruitment Ideas

Looking for new ways to add to your member ranks? Consider these tried-and-tested techniques:

1. Establish a mentoring or adoption program that pairs would-be members with current members.
2. Review your past members and ask them about rejoining.
3. Announce membership updates at each meeting and remind people to bring friends to the next event. Let your members know that recruiting is a top priority for the group.
4. Host a bring-a-friend meeting.
5. Create a bulletin board display in a prominent place showing photos from activities, membership information and a calendar of upcoming events.
6. Seek donations that could be used as incentives to new members who join during your membership drive.
7. Create a membership committee to focus on new ways to bring in members.
8. Hold an informational meeting for prospective members. Ask current members to participate by sharing their reasons for belonging.
9. Pitch a feature article or editorial to your local paper on the successful completion of some member project.
10. Participate in a charity event with another nonprofit or association that will generate added visibility.
11. Survey members about what benefits they deem most valuable. Emphasize these benefits when creating flyers or speaking to potential new members.

76. Junior Associates Circle Targets Under-40 Members

Nonprofits depend on cultivating successive generations of leadership. This is precisely what staff at the Dallas Museum of Art (Dallas, TX) do with their Junior Associates Circle, says Kimberly Bryan, director of donor circle membership.

"Members who support the museum in their 20s and 30s are far more likely to become major donors and trustees as they mature and their resources grow," Bryan says. "It's a way to plan for the future."

The Junior Associates Circle aims to ease younger persons into higher levels of support, she says. Restricted to persons under 40 years of age, membership offers many of the benefits of a full $2,000 Associate membership for just $625.

The under-40 level also offers benefits tailored to younger audiences such as special educational opportunities, tours, exhibitions and travel events. The programming schedule features monthly events culminating in the annual Juniors-only black-tie fundraiser, An Affair of the Art.

Now in its 19th year, the Junior Associates Circle is one of the museum's more active groups, says Bryan, with about 400 household memberships — roughly equal to that of the Associates Circle itself.

Targeting younger supporters is not without its challenges, says Bryan. For instance, the demographic is often highly transient, and relationships can easily be lost when supporters relocate in pursuit of careers, marriage or other opportunities.

But outweighing the challenges are the benefits of engaging people at a young age. "For many people, the circle begins an association that can last for decades or sometimes a lifetime," Bryan says.

For organizations looking to target younger demographics, Bryan recommends strong volunteer leadership. "Peer-to-peer interaction," she says, "is definitely the best way to get a younger group going and keep it strong."

Source: Kimberly Camuel Bryan, Director of Donor Circle Membership, Dallas Museum of Art, Dallas TX. Phone (214) 922-1242. E-mail: kbryan@DallasMuseumofArt.org

ARTICLE DESIGNATION KEY: ▨ RECRUITMENT ▨ RETENTION

77. Forms 'Sell' Volunteer Slots to Members, Potential Members

If your organization offers opportunities for members to volunteer, consider online recruitment forms to assist them in sharing their time and expertise.

The Technical Association of the Pulp and Paper Industry (TAPPI) of Norcross, GA, is accomplishing this through two new volunteer recruitment forms on its website designed to encourage more members, new and existing, to volunteer within the TAPPI ranks.

Serving more than 20,000 professionals in the paper, packaging and converting industry, TAPPI is currently testing these two forms intended to encourage volunteer participation among members and identify skill levels as well as need within the TAPPI community.

Rich Lapin, marketing manager for TAPPI, explains the purpose of each of these new forms:

☐ **Blank Volunteer Form** (top right) — This open-ended request to members allows potential member volunteers to raise their hand to become involved, says Rich Lapin, marketing manager for TAPPI. Areas such as experience level, location and division/committee are intentionally left blank for the volunteer to complete. This form offers those new to the industry and recent college graduates the opportunity to participate readily within the organization by offering their new skills through volunteerism. The form is also intended for use by division and committee leaders as a resource to identify current volunteer needs within their division and to place volunteers based on their experience and skill level within the organization. Once a potential volunteer completes this form, committee leaders review his/her skills set and experience to determine where they may best fit within the volunteer realm of the organization.

☐ **Completed Volunteer Form** (right) — This form is intended to "sell" specific volunteer opportunities at the organization by offering detailed descriptions of volunteer posts. The form is also intended to guide division and committee leaders as they prepare for their immediate volunteer needs. These detailed volunteer descriptions include specifics such as the division/committee, volunteer title, number of positions available, time commitment needed, project type, experience level needed, job description and detailed list of benefits for participating. This form most importantly offers a posting date for the opportunity as well as a posting expiration date. A posting date indicates when the position first becomes available and the expiration date is tied to the term of service needed. This allows volunteer coordinating staff to track when a position completes its term of service or the time by which a new volunteer is needed for that office.

Source: Rich Lapin, Marketing Manager, Technical Association of the Pulp and Paper Industry, Norcross, GA. Phone (770) 209-7290. E-mail: rlapin@tappi.org Website: www.tappi.org

Content not available in this edition

91 Ways to Recruit & Retain More Members

78. Help Members Reach Out to Their Friends, Colleagues

What are you doing to help existing members recruit others?

Sometimes it's difficult for members to know just how to go about recruiting friends and colleagues to join an organization: Do they invite them to a function? Should they just get on the phone and ask?

Often a sincerely written note can accomplish much to begin the recruitment process and give the recipient time to consider the positive aspects of joining.

Draft two or three sample notes such as the example shown here that members can use as a guide in crafting their own messages to would-be members.

Once a note has been sent to a prospective member, instruct the member to give the contact a week or two to think about the invitation, then arrange a casual meeting to discuss it further.

> Hi Patty,
>
> I was thinking about you today as I was volunteering at the Art Center. We really have fun. There's a great group of members and so many great benefits from belonging to the Art Center.
>
> I know you're a busy woman, and I certainly don't want to detract from your family time, but I do wish you would give thought to joining us. Because I know you, I think you and your family would find it to be a rewarding experience.
>
> Will you think about that possibility? You know me; I won't push, but I'd like to chat about it in a week or so. I'll call you for lunch.
>
> Barbara Jensen

79. Five Ways to Motivate Recruitment Efforts

Offering members and staff new ways to recruit members will reenergize them while boosting membership sales. If you're finding your membership recruitment waning, try these five ways to ramp up the process and move toward your membership goals:

1. Offer unique incentives for staff to increase their desire to sell memberships. Try offering a prize that allows them to take a day off with pay for selling the most memberships within a specified time frame.

2. Introduce a member-get-a-member program offering members unique incentives for the most memberships obtained. Create a contest that offers the winning member attendance at the next board retreat or free admission to your next gala event.

3. Begin an advertising campaign that offers incredible deals when groups of five or more join your membership together. Publicize your member benefits and the reduced rates you're offering for group enrollment.

4. Create a membership pampering package for new members who join with a buddy. Take the pair on a tour of your nonprofit, sign them up for new membership and then send them on their way with a basket filled with pampering products and a gift certificate for a massage.

5. Contact every former member to offer the opportunity to join as a new member, giving new member incentives. Allow him/her to participate in the member-get-a-member campaign or membership buddy campaign to generate interest and enthusiasm.

Support Member Base With Annual Recruitment Contest

To create a recruitment contest that motivates current members to sign on newcomers:

- Plan the contest and put it in writing. Include details such as contest dates, goals and expectations, including specific guidelines on conduct.
- Promote professional conduct and fair play in all contest communications.
- Set clear and specific rules as to the contest, process of winning and how prizes will be awarded so there is no confusion on the part of contestants.
- To keep the effort going strong year-round, offer quarterly prizes along with the annual grand prize. Post updated results throughout the contest on your website and in newsletters to get more members excited about the challenge.
- Choose and publicize prizes. Coordinate in-kind donations from partner businesses or headquarters. Get enough prizes to offer them quarterly along with a top annual prize for top recruiters to keep members engaged and seeking to win.
- If the prizes are sizable in value, consider seeking legal counsel to review contest guidelines and eliminate questions as to contest rules and regulations.

---

91 Ways to Recruit & Retain More Members

80. 'Pun' Ways to Appreciate Members ▓▓▓

Looking for fun and humorous takes on member appreciation? Consider these ideas from the National Education Association – New Mexico (Santa Fe, NM).

- Give members bananas — "We find you appealing."
- Give new members potted plants — "Come grow with us."
- Give members lunch boxes with "food for thought" messages from your organization.
- Give bags of peanuts for times they are going nuts (especially good for industry-difficult times of the year like tax day for accountants or semester end for teachers).
- Give members "Thanks a latte" gift coupons.
- Give members microwave popcorn packets — "Things are poppin' in our association."

Source: National Education Association – New Mexico, Santa Fe, NM. Phone (505) 982-1916. Website: www.nea-nm.org

81. Offer a Variety of Member Recognition Awards ▓▓▓

Done right, member award programs can be a powerful way to create motivation and enthusiasm. But moving past the most basic (and often lackluster) awards can be challenging.

The Marketing Research Association (Glastonbury, CT) offers a number of well-conceived membership awards. This sampling gives an idea of creative and meaningful awards an organization can adopt, along with detailed nomination guidelines:

Distinguished Service Award: Recognizes extensive and distinguished service of an individual to both the Marketing Research Association (MRA) and the opinion and marketing research profession. Guidelines:

1. The Distinguished Service Award is a one-time award.
2. Nominations for this award are made by any member, in good standing, at large.
3. Candidates must meet the following criteria:
   a. Is a current member in good standing of MRA.
   b. Has been a national member volunteer for at least five years.
   c. Has demonstrated chapter, national and industry experience.

Chapter of the Year Award: Recognizes one chapter that has not only met all chapter standards set by National, but has exceeded them by obtaining the highest average retention and recruitment rates of all chapters for the chapter board year. Guidelines:

1. The Chapter of the Year Award can be won multiple times.
2. The Chapter of the Year Award is awarded to one chapter each year at MRA's Annual Conference in June. All chapter standards must be met to be considered for this award. The chapter with the highest average of recruitment and retention rates of the chapter board year will win the award. On the rare occasion that average percentages of growth and retention are equal for two (or more) chapters, a tie will result and more than one chapter will be awarded for that year. All official officers on the chapter board will be recognized.
3. There are no nominations for this award. National will select the winning chapter(s) based on National's records of all chapters.

Rising Star Award: Each year, MRA recognizes one or more of its members who have provided outstanding volunteer efforts at the national level for less than five years. Guidelines:

1. The Rising Star Award is a one-time award.
2. The Rising Star Award may be awarded to more than one volunteer each year at the MRA First Outlook Conference.
3. Nominations for this award are made by the general membership of the MRA.
4. Candidates must meet the following criteria:
   a. Is a current member in good standing of the association who is a new MRA volunteer.
   b. Is a National member who has a proven record of outstanding volunteer efforts.
   c. Makes a difference and energetically supports organization at the national level.

Best Educational Offering by a Chapter Award: Recognizes a chapter that has provided an outstanding educational event in the past year. Guidelines:

1. The Best Educational Award can be won multiple times.
2. A call for nominees shall be sent to each chapter board at least one month prior to the close of nominations.
3. A Best Educational Offering Award Chair shall be appointed by the chapter president, who will then assemble a committee responsible for submitting that chapter's nomination(s). A maximum of two nominations per chapter will be accepted. All members significantly involved in putting the event together will receive recognition, up to, but not exceeding, 10 members.
4. Educational events shall be nominated by the chapter board.
5. Educational Offering nominations must meet the following criteria:
   a. Be a non-joint chapter educational event.
   b. Be an event open to all members.

Source: The Marketing Research Association, Glastonbury, CT. Phone (860) 682-1000. Website: www.mra-net.org

---

ARTICLE DESIGNATION KEY: ▓▓▓ RECRUITMENT ▓▓▓ RETENTION

82. Three Steps to Better Renewal Notices

Creating effective renewal notices is an important component of membership retention. Renewal notices need to draw attention and incite action by the member. Follow these three tips to creating better renewal notices:

1. Create stages for your renewal slips. Design six to 10 renewal notices, each with unique copy. Print each on a different color. Then send one each month starting with at least one month prior to the member's renewal date. The new color and fresh copy will draw your members' attention, encouraging them to take notice and take action for renewal.

2. On each renewal slip, highlight a unique or new member benefit to show members the value of renewal. Include information on how to renew and make this process as simple as possible, such as offering a toll-free number or simple online option for renewal by credit card. Include the option of automatic renewal at that time.

3. Create envelopes for each renewal mailing that are colors other than white so the mailing stands out among your members' everyday mail. Have text printed on the envelope that offers a special deal for renewal or alerts the recipient of an urgent reason to open the letter. Avoid red or green envelopes in December so your mailer isn't competing with holiday cards.

83. Sweeten the Pot With New Member Benefits

Freebies can be the shiny penny that turns people's heads toward your organization and entices them to want to learn more.

While advertisers have long known that people like to get more than they paid for, increasing numbers of member organizations are capitalizing on the universal desire by offering special benefits to first-time members.

"They are an enticement, but they also answer a question," says Kristin Gregory, executive director of the Carbondale (IL) Chamber of Commerce, of the complimentary benefits her organization has long provided to new members. "They are a tangible answer to the question of how the chamber serves its members in practical ways."

The chamber's benefits to new members (see box, below) provide something for everyone, but give particular attention to the needs of new or newly relocated business owners, says Gregory. Advertising services, free business consultations and discounted members' services are consistently popular with new members, but chamber officials are always seeking new ideas from both current members and members of the chamber's board of directors.

Though membership incentives are directed primarily toward recruiting new members, current members benefit from these incentives, too. By donating benefits — most of the chamber's incentives are provided by current members — businesses raise awareness of their services and make positive connections with professionals who may become clients.

While few if any members join the chamber expressly to take advantage of first-time benefits, the incentives do help attract potential members and encourage them to sign on, says Gregory. "They are a bonus that adds value in members' minds, and for that we're glad to offer them. It's just another way to show that we're doing whatever we can for members."

Source: Kristin Gregory, Executive Director, Carbondale Chamber of Commerce, Carbondale, IL. Phone (618) 549-2146. E-mail: kristingregory@gmail.com

New Member Benefits Offered By Carbondale (IL) Chamber of Commerce

- ☐ $100 free advertising in The Southern Illinoisan with purchase of $100
- ☐ Free commercial production with placement of advertising schedule on WPSD-TV
- ☐ 25 percent off purchase of advertising from one of the Wither's Radio stations
- ☐ Free business consultation with Feirich/Mager/Green/Ryan Law Firm
- ☐ 30 minutes free business counseling by Gilbert, Huffman, Prosser, Hewson & Barke
- ☐ Free mailbox for one year at Mail Boxes Etc.
- ☐ $0 down, $39.99 dues at Gold's Gym
- ☐ Buy 1 get 1 half price Annual Banquet Tickets (Limit 1)
- ☐ 1 free insert in "The Communicator"
- ☐ 1 free Monthly Member Luncheon Ticket
- ☐ 1 free member list or mailing labels

ARTICLE DESIGNATION KEY: RECRUITMENT RETENTION

91 Ways to Recruit & Retain More Members

84. Recruiting Members — FCCLA Style

Family, Career and Community Leaders of America (FCCLA) of Reston, VA, has a national membership of more than 220,000 young men and women in nearly 7,000 chapters. This nonprofit national career and technical student organization in family and consumer sciences education recruits youth from public and private schools through 12th grade.

Buoying recruitment and retention efforts is the organization's philosophy that members should do much more than simply pay dues — they should get involved.

To grow membership as FCCLA has, follow the organization's 10 Ground Rules for Recruitment Success:

1. **Focus on friendliness.** People get involved in groups that make them feel welcome and involved. Work to create positive, warm, working relationships among all chapter members and potential members.

2. **Make it your job.** Strong chapter membership depends on every member's participation. Strong national membership depends on every chapter's participation. You are a walking billboard for your chapter and the organization. Everything you do and say affects membership.

3. **Ask!** Often the most effective way to get someone to join your chapter is to personally invite him/her to get involved. Don't be shy — speak up and ask people to try your nonprofit.

4. **Ask everyone.** Don't assume others are not interested in joining your chapter. Give them a chance!

5. **Make membership a part of everything.** Every chapter meeting, project and activity influences who joins and stays involved in your chapter. Find ways to strengthen membership with each chapter action.

6. **Know what to say.** Always be ready to explain your organization and what you personally get out of belonging to it. Have this information on the tip of your tongue. Look for every opportunity to talk positively about your chapter and the organization.

7. **Expand your focus.** Design activities to reach new members as well as people who may have drifted away from the group.

8. **Think long term.** You're planning for membership now, but that's not the end of the story. Look for ways current chapter members can leave a legacy of strong membership. Build a positive image among younger members and the community.

9. **Get results!** Plan to strengthen membership numbers, but make sure your efforts get results (more members), not just attention. Make it easy to sign up and pay dues.

10. **Decide who will do what, then do it.** Create to-do lists and ideas for building membership strength. Use these resources as tools to organize, carry out and earn recognition for your membership efforts.

Source: Bana Yahnke, Director of Marketing and Membership, Family, Career and Community Leaders of America, Reston, VA. Phone (703) 476-4900. E-mail: byahnke@fcclainc.org

Top Five Ways to Keep Members

When you have nearly a quarter million members, retention efforts are more important than ever.

So staff with 220,000-member Family, Career and Community Leaders of America (FCCLA) of Reston, VA — a nonprofit national career and technical student organization that recruits youth from public and private schools through 12th grade — get creative to keep members coming back.

Bana Yahnke, director of marketing and membership for FCCLA, shares five ideas that help keep members while strengthening the member-based organization:

❑ **Create a chapter "by the members, for the members, and of the members."** Create a membership that is not just something you join, it's something you do. Make sure members help choose and create chapter projects and activities. The whole chapter determines and pursues these activities together. Discover and use all members' talents and capabilities. Support members' individual projects, and encourage each member to participate in leadership opportunities.

❑ **Give members information and help them get involved.** Chapter leaders, including officers and the advisors, are responsible for knowing what opportunities are available at your organization and offering them to members.

❑ **Create and carry out a program of work.** A program of work is a complete plan for chapter action throughout the year. It spells out the chapter's goals along with the steps members will take to reach them. By writing out a program of work, chapter leaders can analyze the year's plans and make sure there is a balance of team building, fundraising, fun and recognition activities. A written program of work also shows all members what opportunities are available and how they might become involved.

❑ **Know and care about members as individuals.** No one stays involved when he/she stays a stranger. Part of the joy of membership is making connections with other people, especially ones you might not get to know otherwise. Set up a system to have experienced members mentor new members and help them become active in the chapter.

❑ **Plan exciting meetings.** Chapter meetings unify the chapter, accomplish chapter business and inform members about important topics that relate to current chapter projects. Strengthen your chapter's meetings by having a purpose and agenda for the meeting; making sure leaders plan, prepare for and lead the meeting; involving members in making decisions, sharing ideas, asking questions, etc.; and including fun team-building activities.

85. Six Online Survey Tools for Gauging Member Satisfaction ▪▪▪

Touching base with members to gauge their overall satisfaction with your organization is the best way to determine satisfaction of your membership base. Consider the following online survey tools to test the waters of your membership:

- Key Survey (www.keysurvey.com)
- Zoomerang (www.Zoomerang.com)
- Snap Surveys (www.SnapSurveys.com)
- Survey Share (www.surveyshare.com)
- Survey Gold (www.surveygold.com)
- Survey Square (www.surveysquare.com)

Research these and other survey sites for tools you need to evaluate member satisfaction. Take into consideration the survey length, timeliness, mode of transmission and frequency to choose the online survey tool that best suits your needs.

86. How to Write a Winning Membership Renewal Letter ▪▪▪

When sending this year's membership letters, change more than just the date. Review and update the letter's content to boost results.

Think of the communications piece as a retention and renewal letter, not just a renewal letter, says Bunnie Riedel, president of Riedel Communications (Columbia, MD).

"Membership organizations face attrition rates of up to 25 percent," says Riedel, "so your primary goal is to retain as many members as possible. And you do that by communicating why members absolutely have to renew their membership; why no one else can do for them what you do."

The first question an organization must answer in the letter, she says, is "What have you done for me lately?" Articulate the services you have provided in the past year, and explain why those services are valuable. Next, explain what you will do in the immediate future by showcasing benefits members will receive in the coming year or, better yet, next few months.

Only after fulfilling those two components should your letter make the pitch, says Riedel. At this point, don't be shy about asking members to renew memberships or suggesting higher levels of membership, if available.

But the letter, and it should be a letter — Riedel characterizes e-mail renewal campaigns as "a colossal waste of time" — should make members feel necessary and needed. "It should be tight and pressing," she says. "It should convey a sense of immediacy that makes members feel like the money they give is responsible for the survival of the institution; because it is."

A big mistake Riedel sees in such efforts is confining them to a single communication. "Start in advance," she advises. "If membership is due in August, start sending letters in May and have them go every few weeks. It doesn't matter if they are similar in content. The important thing is that they make renewal a priority in members' minds."

Source: Bunnie Riedel, President, Riedel Communications, Inc., Columbia, MD. Phone (410) 992-4976. E-mail: Info@riedelcommunications.com. Website: http://www.riedelcommunications.com

Practical Tips for Renewal Letters

Content is king, but nuts-and-bolts logistics can have real consequences, both positive and negative. These tips on practical considerations are excerpted from "Writing an Effective Membership Renewal Letter" by Bunnie Riedel, president, Riedel Communications (Columbia, MD).

❏ "Try not to go over two pages...I recommend two one-sided pages so it has some weight, but if your organization is highly concerned about conservation, you can do a double sided letter."

❏ "Include a return envelope. You don't have to provide postage and in fact, I recommend you do not provide postage as some will view that as waste. If they really like you, they will spring for the stamp."

❏ "Be sure the outside envelope has 'Address Correction Requested.' While you have to pay the return postage, in the long run it helps keep your list clean."

❏ "Don't forget to include the membership application."

❏ "Be sure the signature of the Executive Director or Chair is in blue, not black. Even while most people understand that the membership letters are computer-generated, having the signature in blue makes it look more personal."

❏ "Be sure to send a thank-you note, it can be brief, but acknowledge their membership."

87. Recruit With a Personal Touch

The American Society for Clinical Laboratory Science (AS-CLS), Bethesda, MD, recruits members using a personal touch.

Sherry Miner, coordinator for membership services at the 8,400-member professional association, shares some of her most successful recruitment methods:

✓ Encourage supervisors to become active members, leading by example. For example, if a laboratory manager is a member of ASCLS, it's more likely that staff members of that laboratory will become active members too.

✓ Have members personally invite nonmembers to meetings to interest more people to join. Encourage members to invite colleagues and friends in the field as a great start to ramping up membership.

✓ Explain benefits of being a member in a professional organization to nonmembers in an informal setting such as a coffee or lunch break.

Source: Sherry Miner, Coordinator, Membership Services, American Society for Clinical Laboratory Science, Bethesda, MD. Phone (301) 657-2768. E-mail: sherrym@ascls.org

88. Develop a Membership Marketing Plan

Creating a formal membership marketing plan is critical to achieving your membership goals, especially in this tough economy, says Ginger Nichols, certified association executive, founder and president of GinCommGroup (Rowlett, TX), which provides consulting services and training to membership associations.

Nichols says a membership marketing plan should not only define your recruitment goals, it should also define your retention ambitions. She recommends including the following sections when creating your membership recruitment and retention plan:

❑ **Key planning assumptions:** An effective membership marketing plan must take into account what is happening in the profession or industry and in the marketplace in which its members and prospective members operate. Making these assumptions explicit provides a benchmark against which to evaluate the continued relevance of the plan. Changes in key assumptions should trigger an examination of the strategies and tactics of the plan.

❑ **Market definition and segmentation:** What is the composition of your market? Analyze demographics of the potential market and compare it to the current universe of members to learn what kinds of members you currently attract and which kinds of prospects you are not reaching. Market segmentation is defined as breaking down the market into smaller, more homogenous groups with similar needs that the organization can successfully satisfy. Target marketing is developing and implementing a specific marketing strategy aimed at a selected segment of the market. This section of the plan should spell out and analyze proposed market segments, determining the fit between the organization's value proposition and its priority market segments.

❑ **Competition:** Once you determine the fit between your organization's capabilities and market needs, consider the other offerings in the marketplace, comparing how your organization's benefits, products and services stack up against the competition.

❑ **Positioning and value proposition:** Positioning is the overall identity the organization projects to differentiate itself from competitors and define its value to members. Positioning should establish a competitive advantage that is reinforced throughout the organization's communications and activities.

❑ **Marketing strategies and tactics:** Nichols defines this section as the nitty-gritty of the plan. Strategies are the broad approaches that will be used; tactics are the specific activities that implement the strategies.

To maximize membership potential, Nichols says, include three broad types of membership strategies — proactive, activity-driven and responsive. Proactive efforts are initiatives specifically aimed at generating new members, such as peer recruitment. Activity-driven approaches link recruitment incentives to other services or programs, such as meeting attendance or program participation. Responsive activities are those designed to close the sale among those who contact the association for membership information.

Include in each strategy an objective, information on how you will track and evaluate your progress and the strategy's cost.

Source: Ginger Nichols, Founder and President, GinCommGroup Consulting & Training for Associations, Rowlett, TX. Phone (972) 463-1824. E-mail: gnichols@gincomm.com. Website: www.gincomm.com

91 Ways to Recruit & Retain More Members

89. Get Volunteers to Help Build Membership

Volunteers can accomplish wonders when it comes to increasing membership, especially when budget resources are limited. Try these methods:

1. Create a membership competition with incentives for both teams and individuals meeting minimum new member goals.

2. Invite volunteers to host coffees or luncheons at their homes for friends and neighbors.

3. Segment your volunteer base according to various groups — seniors, youth, businesses, etc. — and initiate a series of membership campaigns targeted to like groups (e.g., youth calling on youth).

90. Member Loyalty Cards Create Incentive to Join, Get Involved

Since Jan. 1, 2009, members of the Kirkwood-Des Peres Area Chamber of Commerce (Kirkwood, MO) have earned Chamber Rewards points by attending meetings, paying dues on time, advertising in the chamber newsletter and taking part in other activities.

Points are tracked with the personalized barcode member card system, Scan Me In, (St. Louis, MO) developed by Marilyn Elkin, The Barcode Lady LLC (St. Louis, MO).

Members earning the minimum required points are entered into a monthly drawing where they're eligible to receive one of three prizes valued at $25 or more. At month's end, the total points return to zero so every member begins the new month at the same level. However, total cumulative points are recorded, allowing members the opportunity to win quarterly and one big annual prize.

Chamber staff record member points simply by scanning a member's card with a handheld scanner, then uploading scanned information onto the office computer with specialized software that tallies the points earned.

"By introducing the Chamber Rewards cards, our underlying goal is to increase member retention," says Gina March, vice president of marketing for the chamber. "More importantly, this is a fantastic benefit to our members at no cost."

The card (shown at right) boasts the logo of two major sponsors of the rewards program — the sponsor who purchased the cards on behalf of the chamber; and the sponsor donating the first annual grand prize of a furnace and installation ($2,300 value).

The card can also be used to provide member-to-member discounts at member businesses and discounts at participating restaurants. March says both of these added-value benefits work toward the chamber's goal of having members bring at least 5 percent of their purchasing back to the community.

The program has been easy to implement, March says: "It's the easiest thing to get sponsors for the prizes because they get to draw the name of the winners and award the prizes themselves. It's all about giving members exposure."

March also created a prize catalog to coincide with the rewards program, offering another outlet for members to advertise their businesses.

Sources: Marilyn Elkin, The Barcode Lady LLC, St. Louis, MO. Phone (314) 821-1400.
E-mail: MidwestMarking@earthlink.net
Gina March, Vice President of Marketing, Kirkwood-Des Peres Area Chamber of Commerce, Kirkwood, MO.
Phone (314) 821-4161. E-mail: gina@thechamber.us

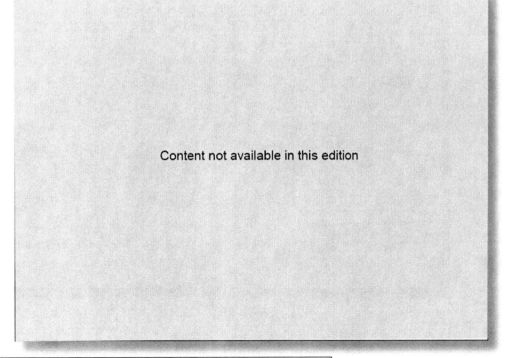

Content not available in this edition

Article Designation Key: ▨ Recruitment ▨ Retention

91. Offer Incentives to Join Beyond the Typical Top 10

While Top 10 lists catch attention, the Pasadena Chamber of Commerce (Pasadena, CA) more than doubles that by giving 21 reasons to join, which is helping to spur membership growth, says Paul Little, chamber president and CEO of the 1,500-member organization.

"In putting together our 21 reasons," Little says, "we boiled the benefits of joining down to bullet points and added some items that are unique to our chamber. We also ranked the items in a way that seem to be most important to our members and potential members."

Source: Paul Little, President and CEO, Pasadena Chamber of Commerce, Pasadena, CA. Phone (626) 795-3355. E-mail: Paul@ pasadena-chamber.org. Website: www.pasadena-chamber.org

The Pasadena Chamber of Commerce (Pasadena, CA) website features this list of 21 reasons to join.

Content not available in this edition